HAZARDOUS CROSSCURRENTS

THE DEVOLUTION REVOLUTION

A series of Century Foundation Reports that analyzes the impact of the widespread shift of government responsibilities from the national to the state and local level.

OTHER REPORTS IN THE SERIES INCLUDE:

CAN THE STATES AFFORD DEVOLUTION? The Fiscal Implications of Shifting Federal Responsibilities to State and Local Governments by *Harold A. Hovey*

MEDICAID AND THE STATES by *Paul Offner*

The Devolution Revolution

Hazardous Crosscurrents

Confronting

Inequality in

an Era of

Devolution

John D. Donahue

A CENTURY FOUNDATION REPORT

1999 • The Century Foundation Press • New York

The Century Foundation, formerly the Twentieth Century Fund, sponsors and supervises timely analyses of economic policy, foreign affairs, and domestic political issues. Not-for-profit and nonpartisan, it was founded in 1919 and endowed by Edward A. Filene.

Cataloging in Publication Data

Donahue, John D.
    Hazardous crosscurrents : confronting inequality in an era of devolution / John D. Donahue.
        p. cm. -- (Devolution revolution)
    Includes bibliographical references (p.   ) and index.
    ISBN 0-87078-428-5
    1. Federal Government--United States.   2. Central-local government relations--United States.   3. Intergovernmental fiscal relations--United States.   4. Income distribution--United States.   I. Title.   II. Series.
JK325.D67   1998
351.73--dc21   98–41540
                                                                                CIP

FOREWORD

Robert Putnam's *Making Democracy Work: Civic Traditions in Modern Italy* was one of the most important works of social science of the late twentieth century. The result of twenty-five years of study, it explored, among other things, a range of possible explanations for the dramatically differing performances of the regional government structures put in place in Italy beginning in 1970. Putnam drew many important conclusions from his study, including the widely cited observation that significant differences in civic culture, some nearly a thousand years in the making, appear to be highly correlated with the relative success or failure of these experiments in subnational government.

Since Putnam's book appeared, there have been numerous attempts to apply his approach to the American context. But I know of no evidence that it was ever discussed during the scramble to "devolve" substantial national responsibilities to the fifty states. Indeed, in the United States the diversity among the states, both real and imaginary, is more celebrated than studied. But what does it mean for the provision of public services? Certainly it is no cause for jubilation that infant mortality ranges from 10.5 per 1,000 live births in Mississippi to 5.2 in Massachusetts. Nor can the wide gulf between the highest-performing states in elementary and secondary education and the bottom tier be the result of conscious preferences for diversity.

Today, because of the movement to give the states a larger role in such programs as Medicaid, welfare, and housing, these questions have taken on a new importance. For the one sure consequence of devolution is that it will result in a wider range of administrative arrangements, means of intervention, and levels of assistance for citizens affected by these programs. Given this, the Trustees of The Century Foundation decided that serious research and analysis on the impact of devolution could be of real value to policymakers and the public. We asked Carol Kellerman, former chief of staff to Senator Charles Schumer when he was a member of Congress and now executive director of the New York City School Volunteer Program, to help us edit a series of reports on specific areas where change was under way.

In this volume, John D. Donahue, associate professor of public policy at Harvard's John F. Kennedy School of Government, explores possible connections between the trends toward greater economic inequality and toward more state-centered government. Without claiming that devolution of authority from the federal level to the states is responsible for widening the gaps between the rich and poor, Donahue does argue that devolution has made it more difficult to offset the economic forces that have produced greater inequality. He explores particular realms of public policy—taxation, antipoverty programs, education, and job training—to demonstrate the relatively limited capacity of states collectively to keep low-income families from falling further behind. As a former assistant secretary of the U.S. Labor Department during the first term of the Clinton administration, Donahue saw firsthand how limited the federal government's powers had become.

Other reports in this series include *Can the States Afford Devolution? The Fiscal Implications of Shifting Federal Responsibilities to State and Local Governments* by Harold A. Hovey, president of State Policy Research Inc. and the editor of its newsletters, *State Policy Reports* and *State Budget and Tax News*; *Medicaid and the States* by Paul Offner, commissioner of health care finance for the District of Columbia; and *Housing Policy and Devolution* by Peter Dreier, director of the public policy program at Occidental College.

We thank Donahue for his thoughtful examination of this aspect of the many issues involved in devolution.

RICHARD C. LEONE, *President*
The Century Foundation
April 1999

PREFACE

The framers of the U.S. Constitution and the Bill of Rights bequeathed a riddle in the form of the countervailing aims of the Supremacy Clause and the Tenth Amendment (reserving powers not expressly given to Washington for the states), and Americans have been trying to solve it ever since. The proper balance of power between national and state governments has been the topic of endless argument throughout our country's history as policymakers have tried to get the workings of "federalism" just right.

In the early years, states enjoyed far more legitimacy and authority than the distant national government. Some of the ambiguities of the federal system were resolved in favor of national unity by the Supreme Court's decisions in *McCulloch* v. *Maryland* (1816) and *Gibbons* v. *Ogden* (1824). Then, at mid-century, the clash between states' rights and the Union over slavery became so severe that only war could settle it. The Civil War and Reconstruction period, in which the federal government virtually occupied the defeated southern states and three new constitutional amendments were adopted, represented a vast shift of power away from state capitols.

The New Deal was another period of unprecedented central government activism, reinforced by the massive national mobilization required for World War II. The prosperity of the first postwar decades seemed to affirm the wisdom of a strong federal hand at the economic helm. Later, the struggle for civil rights echoed the rhetoric and the policy imperatives of Reconstruction. "States' rights" took on negative connotations as federal marshals marched into recalcitrant states to open schoolhouse doors to African Americans.

The power of Washington in domestic affairs reached its high-water mark in the early 1970s. The Great Society had created hundreds of new "categorical" programs to be administered locally but subject to federal policy guidelines, rules, and regulations. Federal funding for these categorical programs grew from $7.7 billion in 1962 to $41.7 billion in 1973. State and local governments were cast as the federal government's agents or subcontractors; Washington now played a role in virtually every public function in every state.

Then, two Republican presidents, under the banner of a "New Federalism" started to move the balance of power in the other direction. Nixon's new federalism was an effort to shift the Great Society's categorical grants to block grants, funded by Washington but controlled at the local level in the form of general revenue sharing. Reagan's new federalism was a far more aggressive repudiation of centralized power. Instead of providing resources while ceding control, Reagan, a former governor, sought to renounce the federal government's fiscal responsibility for large areas of public policy.

Under Reagan, more than five hundred categorical programs were consolidated into nine block grants. General revenue sharing, the hallmark of Nixon's new federalism, had disappeared by 1986. Overall, transfers from Washington to the states and cities declined, and the locus of control for block grants became state governments, not cities or local community organizations.

President Clinton, of course, came into office with the reputation and instincts of an innovative governor and had considerable sympathy with the view from the states. But before his agenda for federalism could clearly emerge, the 1994 elections brought a new cast to the 104th Congress, decidedly in favor of those with experience in government at the state level: there were seventeen former governors and thirty-eight former state representatives in the Senate, and nearly half of the members of the House had previous service in state legislatures. Moreover, the number of Republican governors leapt from nineteen to thirty-one in a single election year. There was now a critical mass of fresh leaders at the state level—thirsty for authority, unified in how they would deploy it, and in sync with their congressional delegations and the new Republican majority in Washington.

These advocates of state primacy found their voice and issued a clarion call—for "devolution." Proponents of devolution promise greater efficiency, cost savings, and innovation as power moves closer to the people, and this faith in "power to the people" is enjoying as much of a consensus as American politics ever allows.

The tide of authority and resources is now flowing away from Washington and toward the states. A Democratic president and members on both sides of the aisle in Congress enthusiastically supported a law prohibiting the imposition of "unfunded mandates" on the states; other legislation passed in the 1990s has expanded state discretion over transportation spending, drinking water standards, and highway safety.

Then came welfare "reform," the most vivid example of the devolution movement. A sixty-year tradition of federal responsibility for antipoverty programs was repudiated in one fell swoop, replaced by freestanding state programs whose character and effectiveness will emerge only over time. Meanwhile, the Supreme Court also has shown evidence of a historic tilt in favor of state authority, throwing out such seemingly straightforward exercises of centralized control as the requirement that local law enforcement personnel administer a seven-day waiting period on handgun purchases.

What are the underlying causes of the devolution trend?

One is that Americans' current disenchantment with the federal government does not seem to extend as strongly to their states and localities. During the Depression, a 1936 Gallup poll found that 56 percent of Americans favored concentrating power in the federal government, but contemporary opinion surveys indicate that most people have little confidence in the federal government, believing states and localities can do a better job of running most things.

Another explanation is that states and localities have been slowly but surely occupying a large and growing share of the fiscal terrain as Washington retrenches. Federal spending on everything other than defense, income transfers, and interest payments averaged 3.6 percent of the economy in the 1970s but has dropped back to an average of 2.2 percent in the 1990s and was only 1.5 percent in 1997. Meanwhile, state and community spending from revenues generated at the local levels has continued to climb; it is now seven times as large as the federal share.

Not surprisingly, human resources are moving in the same direction. While federal civilian employment has been declining to the point where it is now barely 1 percent of the population, state and local employment has reached almost 17 million—well exceeding 6 percent of the population. Statehouse politics is no longer considered minor league. Many ambitious Democrats and Republicans have dedicated themselves to careers in state and city government, and the profile of state activism has risen to the point that governors and former governors are among the most prominent, thoughtful, and articulate leaders in both major parties.

To be sure, there is something to be said for Justice Brandeis's oft-repeated description of the states as policy "laboratories" that test and winnow policy alternatives, providing the country with valuable information about what works and what does not. Indeed, there may be value in diversity itself. Since citizens and corporations differ in their priorities, the nation may be better off if there is a range of alternative packages of services, regulatory regimes, and tax burdens among the states from which voters and those with influence on policy can choose.

But the shift toward state-based government entails trade-offs and may carry fundamental and far-reaching consequences for our economy and culture that have yet to be fully recognized. The papers in this series attempt to explore those complexities, getting beyond the upbeat rhetoric of "power to the people" to examine how devolution affects real world decisions in specific areas of policy. Rather than accept without challenge the premise that authority is always better exercised at smaller levels of government, the series' authors assess the impact of devolving issues of vital importance to Americans—economic inequality, Medicaid, and housing policy.

As the world's economy becomes more integrated and more unforgivingly competitive, a fragmented American public sector may seriously hurt our prospects for narrowing economic disparities and preserving a largely middle-class society. These papers sound a clear warning of the dangers we face if the balance of power shifts too heavily in the prevailing direction.

CAROL KELLERMAN
Executive Director
New York City School Volunteer Program

Contents

1

INTRODUCTION

Americans have been growing apart for roughly a generation, as deepening economic disparities erode our sense of common prospects. At the same time, we have been turning away from Washington and toward the separate states for solutions to our public problems. Trends marking the final fifth of the twentieth century in the United States include both a shift in the public sector's center of gravity outward from the federal government, and an increasingly unequal distribution of income.

The upper line of Figure 1.1 (see page 2) traces self-funded state and local spending as a fraction of domestic public spending other than the "check-writing" functions—Social Security, Medicare, and debt service—that now claim the bulk of the federal budget. The lower line measures the share of total family income collected by the most affluent 20 percent. While the trajectories differ in detail,* both indicators, through economic boom and bust and through the cycles of political seasons, have remained well above their 1980 levels. And neither seems poised to retreat.

---

* The shift toward subnational government since 1980 has been sharper; income concentration has slowed, while the state and local share of public spending has continued its climb.

FIGURE 1.1 STATE AND LOCAL SHARE OF DOMESTIC PUBLIC SPENDING (EXCLUDING SS, MEDICARE, INTEREST) AND UPPER-FIFTH SHARE OF FAMILY INCOME (INDEX: 1980 = 100)

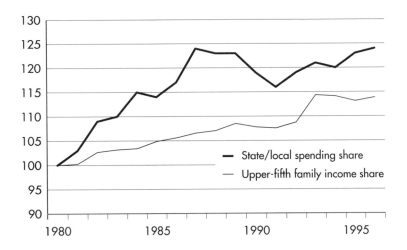

Sources: Spending data calculated from U.S. Office of Management and Budget, *Budget of the United States Government Fiscal Year 1998* (Washington, D.C.: U.S. Government Printing Office, 1997), Historical Table 15.4 (www.access.gpo.gov/su_docs/budget98/his15z4); income data calculated from U.S. Department of Commerce, Bureau of the Census, *Detailed Historical Tables from the Current Population Survey (CPS) 1947–1996*, Table F-3, "Mean Income Received by Each Fifth and Top 5 Percent of Families (All Races): 1966 to 1996" (www.census.gov/hhes/income/histinc/f03).

Coincident trends, to be sure, prove nothing on their own. The fraction of families with home computers and the proportion of political advertisements with a negative theme also have risen roughly in parallel since 1980, and few would suggest a causal link. Nor is there much reason to anticipate some *simple* relationship between governmental decentralization and income inequality. But it is striking that at a point in our history when Americans' economic fates diverge to a degree that few now living have ever witnessed—and when we must choose whether to push back against this trend or make our peace with it—we are increasingly confronting our common challenges, not nationally, but rather state by state. This essay describes both government's shift toward the states and the growth in inequality that characterize the end of this century, and then speculates on some implications for the choices awaiting us in the next.

2

ECONOMIC INEQUALITY:
HOW IT'S GROWN, WHY IT MATTERS

U ntil recently, "inequality" was a code word in American political
discourse for the special problems of the poor (and especially the
minority poor) left behind by the great middle-class boom of the early
postwar decades. Those problems are still with us. But economic
inequality has become something far broader than vestigial poverty
amid generally shared prosperity. The pervasive economic fragmentation that began toward the end of the 1970s, if it follows a similar
path for a similar period, would bequeath to the next generation
(instead of America's cherished heritage as a relatively classless society) an economic structure more reminiscent of Victorian England
or modern Latin America. Class conventions displayed in movies
from the 1930s, which twenty years ago seemed far removed from
modern American realities, no longer appear quite so antique.

There are many ways to measure income inequality. The most
common statistical metric is the Gini coefficient, an index ranging from zero to one, which has the virtue of expressing income
dispersion in a single number but the disadvantage of defying
intuition. (Both extreme values of the Gini coefficient are straightforward: 0.0 means everybody has exactly the same income; 1.0
means a single individual has *all* the income and everyone else is

penniless. But values of the Gini coefficient actually encountered, mostly in the 0.2 to 0.5 range, are harder to translate into intuitively meaningful terms.) A less refined but more accessible measure focuses on the shares of total income accruing to varying fractions of the population.

Each March, platoons of Census Bureau researchers conduct large-scale surveys of American residents that cover (among other things) income earned in the previous year.[1] This Current Population Survey (CPS) employs a broad definition of income, including not only wages and salaries but also public assistance and Social Security payments, alimony, interest and dividends, and so on. It doesn't cover quite everything. For example, the buying power of very poor respondents is understated somewhat by the omission of food stamps, subsidized housing, and other forms of assistance that aren't delivered as cash. At the other end of the spectrum, the CPS misses most capital gains, and it records respondents' earnings in a way that understates very large incomes. But the CPS does a fairly good job of capturing what most people think of as income. (Alternative definitions that adjust for taxes, noncash transfers, noncash returns on capital and real estate, and other factors show different aspects of income distribution at any single point in time, but don't change the trends in any major way.)

Income data based on the Current Population Survey are conventionally broken down into "quintiles," showing the share of income earned by the bottom fifth, the next fifth, the middle, next-to-top, and the top fifth. The very top 5 percent is often singled out from the rest of the upper quintile. Income data are collected for "families," defined as two or more related people living together, and for "households," a broader category that includes not just families but also people living alone and unrelated people sharing a home.

Table 2.1 shows the 1996 income picture for America's 101 million households, based on CPS data collected in March 1997. Table 2.2 shows the comparable view for America's 70 million *families*— essentially a more restricted take on the same data, leaving out people living alone and households made up of people who aren't related by birth or marriage or adoption.

Since the typically lower incomes of people living alone tend to drag down the more inclusive "household" figures, average income for families is higher across the spectrum—a lot higher (33 percent

TABLE 2.1 AMERICAN HOUSEHOLD INCOME, 1996

	Bottom fifth	Second-lowest fifth	Middle fifth	Second-highest fifth	Top fifth (including top twentieth)	(Top twentieth alone)
Average income for these households	$8,596	$21,097	$35,486	$54,922	$115,514	$201,220
Share of all household income	3.7	9.0	15.1	23.3	49.0	21.4

Sources: Average household income by quintile from *Detailed Historical Tables from the Current Population Survey (CPS) 1947–1996*, Table H-3 "Mean Income Received by Each Fifth and Top 5 Percent of Households (All Races): 1967 to 1996" (www.census.gov/hhes/income/histinc/h03); quintile shares of household income from Table H-2, "Share of Aggregate Income Received by Each Fifth and Top 5 Percent of Households (All Races): 1967 to 1996" (www.census.gov/hhes/income/histinc/h02).

TABLE 2.2 AMERICAN FAMILY INCOME, 1996

	Bottom fifth	Second-lowest fifth	Middle fifth	Second-highest fifth	Top fifth (including top twentieth)	(Top twentieth alone)
Average income for these families	$11,388	$26,847	$42,467	$62,052	$125,627	$217,355
Share of all family income	4.2	10.0	15.8	23.1	46.8	20.3

Sources: Average family income by quintile from *Detailed Historical Tables from the Current Population Survey (CPS) 1947–1996*, Table F-3, "Mean Income Received by Each Fifth and Top 5 Percent of Families (All Races): 1966 to 1996" (www.census.gov/hhes/income/histinc/f03); quintile shares of family income from Table F-2, "Share of Aggregate Income Received by Each Fifth and Top 5 Percent of Families (All Races): 1947 to 1996" (www.census.gov/hhes/income/histinc/f02).

and 27 percent respectively) for the bottom two quintiles, which contain relatively more nonfamily households, with progressively less difference between household figures and family figures as you move up the income scale. Inequality is also more pronounced for the household data than for the narrower family data; the bottom fifth has 3.7 percent of total income instead of 4.2 percent; the top twentieth has 21.4 percent instead of 20.3 percent. While the growing number and the relatively low income of nonfamily households summon some real policy issues, those issues aren't central for present purposes. So I concentrate here on family income rather than household income—but do bear in mind that this softens somewhat the picture of income inequality presented.[2]

While the comparisons are necessarily imprecise—income data have been collected, in something like their current form, only since the late 1940s—the last time incomes diverged this widely was in the 1920s, before the upheavals of the Depression, the New Deal, and World War II reshuffled the deck. Figure 2.1 tracks the trends. In a rigidly egalitarian economy—which America never has been and never will be—this figure would display five steady bands of equal width. The actual picture is decidedly different, but what is most interesting is the change over time. From the late 1940s to the early 1950s, as a remarkable postwar wave of shared prosperity gathered force, the top fifth's share of total family income generally ranged between 42 and 43 percent, declining a bit to around 41 percent in the later 1950s. (In other words, the most fortunate one-fifth of the families earned a little more than two-fifths of the income.) For the next generation, through boom and bust, it stayed very close to that level, going no higher than 1961's 42.2 and no lower than 1968's 40.5.

Not until the 1980s did the top fifth's share of family income break out beyond the narrow range it had wandered since the 1950s. But it then staked out a sharp upward course. In 1982 it matched the previous generation's 1961 peak of 42.2 percent; the next year it exceeded it. In 1985 it beat the recorded high of 43 percent. The very next year it climbed another percentage point and continued surging, reaching 47 percent in 1993 and staying since then close to that peak.[3]

Even more remarkable has been the concentration of income at the peak of the income distribution—the top slice of the top slice. From 1953 until 1986, the upper one-twentieth of American families

FIGURE 2.1 FAMILY INCOME DISTRIBUTION, 1947–96

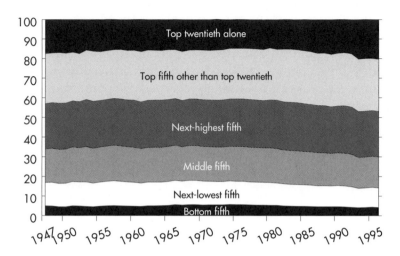

Note: Data freshly released by the Census Bureau as this report went to press show that the trend continued through 1997. The top 5 percent of families collected a postwar record of 20.7 percent of total American family income, increasing their share by 0.4 percent over 1996. The income share of the rest of the top fifth, and that of the bottom fifth, stayed constant; the share of the middle 60 percent declined. *Detailed Historical Tables from the Current Population Survey (CPS) 1947–1997*, Table F-2, "Share of Aggregate IncomeReceived by Each Fifth and Top 5 Percent of Families (All Races): 1947 to 1997" (www.census.gov/hhes/income/histinc/f02, accessed September 25, 1998).

Source: U.S. Department of Commerce, Bureau of the Census, *Detailed Historical Tables from the Current Population Survey (CPS) 1947–1996*, Table F-2, "Share of Aggregate Income Received by Each Fifth and Top 5 Percent of Families (All Races): 1947 to 1996" (www.census.gov/hhes/income/histinc/f02).

earned around 15 or 16 percent of total income, or something like three times what they would have collected under lockstep egalitarianism. In 1987 their share reached 17 percent, and has been around 20 percent since 1993. These might seem like rather modest changes. But for a sense of perspective, consider that the *increase* in the top twentieth's share of family income between 1985 and 1996—an extra 4.2 percent of the total—was as large as the *entire* share of income collected by the bottom one-fifth of American families in 1996.

If the most fortunate families have been getting a larger fraction of total family income, whose share has been falling? The best off have *not* been gaining at the main expense of the worst off, in part due to the simple fact that the bottom fifth has never had much to lose. The lowest quintile collected 5.3 percent of family income in 1980 and 4.2 percent in 1996. Most of the shift came from the middle three-fifths, who collectively claimed 54 percent of family income in 1980—not all that different from their 60 percent of the population—but only 49 percent in 1996. Indeed, what might be termed the upper middle class—the top quintile *excluding* the top twentieth—has just held its own in terms of income share. It garnered 26.5 percent of family income in 1980, and exactly the same share in 1996.

EXPLANATIONS OF RISING INEQUALITY

Why has this growth in inequality occurred? Before turning to some more credible explanations, it may be helpful to dispense with a few popular myths. An article of faith among some on the left is that Reagan-era tax cuts are to blame for surging inequality. But this charge rings hollow. For one thing, the timing is wrong. Incomes started to diverge a few years before the big 1982 cuts in top tax rates, and continued to diverge even after taxes on the wealthiest were raised again in 1986, 1990, and 1993. Even if the tax-cut explanation were plausible in terms of timing, it would confront the fatal objection that the CPS measures *pre*tax income. Unless the tax cuts had an impact on high earners' incentives to work that was extravagantly in excess of what most analysts can credit—and unless the 1982 tax *cuts* boosted upper-income workers' industriousness, but the subsequent *increases* had no countervailing effect—tax policy simply cannot be a major part of the story.[4]

Nor—to address another common charge from the left—have the concentration of wealth and the booming stock market triggered the ascendancy of a *rentier* class whose investment returns vault them ahead of families reliant on mere labor income. While it is true that wages and salaries have fallen from around 66 percent of total personal income through the 1960s to around 56 or 57 percent in the

1990s, this is almost entirely due not to rising capital earnings, but to the growth of transfer payments, from around 7 to around 17 percent of total income. (These transfers are overwhelmingly Social Security and public pensions; "means-tested" benefits account for a minor share of the total.) Earnings from capital (including dividends, rents, interest payments, and profits collected by business owners) ran around a quarter of total income through most of the 1960s and about the same—if anything, a bit lower—in the 1990s.[5] Diverging earning power, rather than the growth of "unearned" income, is the main engine of economic inequality.

A parallel myth, this one cherished by the right, is that growing inequality is canceled out by economic mobility. America's defining ethic of competition and opportunity makes for an ever-changing economic hierarchy, this story goes. The fluidity of the United States' income distribution renders all but irrelevant any single year's lineup of rich and poor, as affluence averages out over time: The man down on his luck one year makes it big the next; the high-earning woman is leap-frogged by eager rivals if she tries to coast. If people slip and slide continuously across the income spectrum, from rags to riches and from riches to rags, then one could argue that the width of that spectrum is a less weighty concern than it might be if the United States shared the Old World's class rigidities. The logic, in the abstract, is surely defensible. And it is true that the Current Population Survey and similar data series *would* miss this sort of averaging out, if it in fact occurred, since they focus narrowly on a single year's income and are blind to respondents' future or past.

But a separate series called the Panel Study of Income Dynamics tracks a consistent sample over time, and thus captures the effects of economic mobility. A study based on PSID data and performed by Peter Gottschalk followed a large group of men in their prime working years from 1974 to 1991.[6] There was certainly enough evidence of shifting fortunes to complicate the inequality picture presented by any single year's survey data. By 1991, nearly 8 percent of those who had been in 1974's bottom fifth (through whatever combination of education, experience, hard work, and good luck) had climbed their way to the top fifth. And 3 percent of those in the top fifth in 1974 had fallen into the bottom fifth.[7] Yet despite these cases of large gains and losses, the basic pattern of inequality is altered only modestly by factoring in mobility. Of those starting out in the lowest quintile, the plurality (42 percent) ended up at the very bottom as well. Even with seventeen years' worth of opportunity, only one in five made it into the upper two-fifths of the income distribution. The top of the distribution showed even less churning; over half of 1974's top quintile were still at the top in 1991, most of the rest were in the next-richest fifth, and only one in ten had fallen to the bottom or the next-to-lowest quintile.

In short, bringing mobility into the picture makes the inequality scenario look a notch or two less stark, but comes nowhere near erasing it. Gottschalk calculates that averaging out earnings over the whole seventeen-year period reduces income inequality by only about one-third, relative to what the snapshot based on a single year's data would suggest.[8] The "opportunity trumps inequality" theme is also undercut by the fact that income mobility in America is not, in fact, very different from the pattern in other OECD countries with far less inequality. In economic terms, at least, the United States is by no means a uniquely fluid society. Nor is there any evidence that mobility has risen over recent years to counterbalance America's growth in inequality.[9]

Finally, some argue that inequality is greatly exaggerated, since conventional measures like the Current Population Survey income figures ignore massive redistribution brought about by taxation and transfer programs. It is true that the federal income tax falls more heavily on high-earning families, as do many (though by no means all) other taxes. And government transfer programs do, on balance, improve the position of the worst off. But taxes and transfers turn out to have a rather modest effect on income distribution, and relying on the plain-vanilla definition of income—pretax, pretransfer—doesn't distort matters much. Alternative definitions of income, employed experimentally by the researchers who run the CPS, take into account federal and state income taxes, Medicare, Medicaid, private health insurance benefits, and government transfer programs (whether means-tested or not, and whether delivered in cash or in kind). Calculations based on these more comprehensive measures of income yield about 90 percent as much income inequality in 1996 as do calculations based on the standard definition. Moreover, inequality has increased since 1980 by *more*, not less, when income is measured in posttax, posttransfer terms.[10]

If inequality isn't the simple product of Reagan tax cuts, or an illusion based on mismeasurement or on static pictures of a dynamic economy, or a matter of the returns to capital outpacing earnings from work, what *is* going on? The backdrop for widening income inequality has been a slowdown in overall growth—a slowdown from which only the top has been spared. In contrast to the robust and broad-based prosperity of the early postwar decades, income growth from the mid-1970s until very recently has been mostly meager. Coupled with uneven distribution, this has meant that between 1980 and 1996 average family income for the bottom fifth, adjusted for inflation, actually *fell* 7 percent. The next highest fifth gained only one percent. Family incomes for the middle fifth grew 6 percent; for the next-to-highest fifth, 11 percent; for the highest fifth, 34 percent; and for the top one-twentieth, 63 percent.[11] The data from which these figures are drawn are criticized frequently, and with some justice, as distorted; the Consumer Price Index used to adjust the yearly figures into dollars of constant purchasing power almost certainly overstates inflation to some degree. But the bias, if any, cuts across the income distribution and is irrelevant to the main point: Americans in the top families, especially the very top, have sprinted away from the rest in the rewards their work can command.

There is no single reason for this divergence in earning power between the top fifth and everyone else, but rather a network of partly interrelated explanations. Some of these explanations have little or nothing to do with the concentration or dispersal of governmental authority, and indeed little or nothing to do with government at all. But as later sections of this essay will explore, some of the factors behind income inequality are intricately linked to the allocation of power and duties across levels of American government.

Family Structure and Roles

A seemingly paradoxical contributor to family income inequality—and one rather remote from questions of federal-state balance—has been America's progress in overcoming gender inequality. We have come very far, in a very short time, from the days when just the poorest families relied much on women's earnings. In the 1960s only a little over one in three adult women worked for pay, versus around 85 percent of adult men; by 1996 the fraction of adult women in the labor force approached 60 percent, while the fraction of adult men had slipped to 77 percent.[12]

American women's exodus from kitchens and nurseries to offices and factories has been widely recognized, its social consequences celebrated by some, lamented by others. Less noted are the implications for family income inequality of women's growing representation in the workforce, coupled with the fact that high-earning women are frequently married to high-earning men, while low-earning women are not infre-quently married to nobody. A disproportionate number of low-income families consist of single working mothers and their children, and the growth of single parenthood is a major factor in family income inequal-ity. At the other end of the spectrum a phenomenon that sociologists (somewhat unromantically) term "assortive mating" comes into play: Americans tend to choose spouses with education levels similar to their own. As the return to education rises and workplace barriers to women fall, this pattern deepens differences in families' overall earning power. One researcher studied data from a large sample of married couples, varying widely in their economic circumstances, over nearly three decades starting in 1960. In the 1980s—unlike the 1960s—the greater a man's earnings, the more his wife tended to earn as well. The lower-earning half of the sample of men would have suffered real declines in family income between 1969 and 1989 had their wives not stepped up their contributions to family finances. (The lowest *fifth* still lost ground, but less than they would have lost if the wives hadn't worked longer and earned more.) For the more affluent half of the men in the sample— and especially the top 10 percent—wives' rising earnings accentuated the effect of husbands' rising earnings.[13] So beyond the cultural impacts of one of this century's most striking trends, it is all but undeniable that women's surge into the workforce has had something to do with diverg-ing family incomes. Yet marriages that unite high earners, and single parenthood or divorces that leave low earners on their own, only ampli-fy the underlying fact that earning power itself is becoming much more uneven.

The gap between the upper and lower reaches of the wage and salary distribution in the United States is wide not only by the standards of our own recent past, but by international standards as well. Two leading researchers for an ambitious cross-national project called the Luxembourg Income Study have looked at the earnings of similar workers (men who work full-time) at similar points in time (the late 1980s or early 1990s) in the seven OECD countries that keep suffi-ciently precise statistics to make comparisons possible. Rather than examining the very top and the very bottom of the earnings distrib-ution (which would risk letting America's extreme cases warp the international comparison) they focus on workers 10 percent up from the bottom, and 10 percent down from the top—the tenth percentile and ninetieth percentile, in analysts' argot. In the United States, those ninetieth-percentile workers (not top executives, medical specialists, or successful entrepreneurs, but more likely run-of-the-mill professionals, middle managers, or experienced technicians) earned 5.7 times as much as tenth-percentile workers. Only in Canada, with a ratio of 4.6, was the gap anywhere near so large. In the other advanced countries studied—Germany, the United Kingdom, the Netherlands, Australia, and Sweden—relatively (but not extremely) well-paid men earned 2.4 to 3.5 times as much as relatively (but not extremely) low-paid men. The dispersal in earning power was so large that even though *average* earnings in the United States exceed average earnings elsewhere, tenth-percentile American men earned less *in absolute terms* than tenth-percentile men in any of the other countries.[14]

The fundamental cause of family income inequality is diverging earning power. This underscores the urgency of determining just why the pay that different workers can command is becoming so much more unequal. A vigorous debate has been raging for years, seeking to pin down the causes of earnings inequality. The usual suspects include trade and immigration, technological progress, and changes in the laws, policies, and institutions that govern the workplace.

Global Market Integration

Over roughly the same period that income gaps have widened, the American economy has become progressively more intertwined with global markets. Imports rose from around 3 percent of GDP in the early 1960s to around 10 percent in the mid-1990s.[15] The foreign-born fraction of the population recorded by the 1970 Census was 4.7 percent; in 1990, the figure was 7.9 percent, plus an unknown but large number of illegal immigrants.[16] Competition from lower-wage workers, by the most elementary sort of economic logic, tends to reduce the earnings of those exposed to the competition. If some Americans face increasing degrees of such rivalry—either because immigrants working in America are willing to do more cheaply the tasks that would otherwise be performed by natives, or because lower-paid workers overseas are willing to make the products or provide the services that otherwise would be produced domestically—while other Americans are more shielded from competition, then globalization will alter the distribution of earning power. And if the workers who are already low-paid turn out to be especially affected by foreign competition, then global integration will worsen wage inequality.[17]

Some portion of the rise in inequality is clearly due to global integration, but analysts raucously disagree about just how large that portion is. Labor economist Richard Freeman judges that immigration and trade together account for at least 5 percent and up to 20 percent of the increase in inequality.[18] His colleague George Borjas sees a somewhat larger effect, with trade accounting for about a quarter of the increase in wage inequality between 1976 and 1990 and immigration causing about a third of high school dropouts' loss in relative earning power from 1980 to 1988.[19] Robert Z. Lawrence, emphasizing that most U.S. trade is with other rich countries, suggests that low-wage competition is a sideshow to the integration of advanced economies. By his reckoning, trade accounts for no more than 10 to 15 percent of the wage gap between high school- and college-educated Americans.[20] Dani Rodrik and others counter that the uneasy knowledge among American workers that they *could* be replaced by foreign alternatives suppresses their wages, even if the threat remains latent. The debate continues. An informal (but nonetheless influential) survey of economists conducted by Alan Krueger and Orley Ashenfelter at a 1995 New York Federal Reserve colloquium found that the group, on average, attributed about 11 percent of the rise in wage inequality to trade and about 7 percent to immigration.[21]

The Shifting Demand for Skills

It is impossible to account for growing inequality without reference to the torrent of technological change that has shriveled demand for unskilled labor and raised the payoff to advanced skills. Just as agriculture gradually faded from economic mainstay to economic marginality, so too (but much more quickly) has manufacturing's relative importance waned.[22] Within the service sector, technological change has spawned new categories of high-skilled occupations in health care, information processing, and business services. Even within the goods-producing sector, new technologies have devalued physical strength and faithful adherence to routine while emphasizing workers' training, flexibility, and initiative. Stepped-up technological evolution offers glittering new opportunities for those in a position to seize them. But those who lack workplace skills, or who placed their career bets on obsolete industrial structures, are left stranded by the new economic tides.

Workers with the right training, and with the educational foundations that equip them to continually improve their skills, discover that new communications and information technologies leverage their ability to create economic value. Employers bid for the services of these high-skilled workers, and their earning power soars. At the same time, however, the penalties for lacking the right skills are becoming harsher. As workers without education find demand evaporating for the kinds of work they can do, their earnings decline both in absolute terms and (even more dramatically) in comparison to their more skilled counterparts.

Consider the evolution of the "education premium"—the extra earning power conferred by higher education—for adult men. Education has always mattered for earnings. But it now matters considerably more that it used to. In 1980, college graduates collected 34 percent more annual personal income, on average, than high school graduates. Men with some postgraduate education, in turn, earned 15 percent more than those who stopped with the bachelor's degree. By 1996, college graduates earned 60 percent more than high school graduates. And men with postgraduate degrees earned 58 percent more than college graduates.[23] In other words, in just sixteen years the best-educated men went from earning roughly one and a half times as much as high school graduates to earning over two and a half times as much.

So dramatic a surge in the payoff for postsecondary education, over so short a period, attests to the force of the technological trends that have been raising the demand for skilled labor. Yet the widening of the education premium is even more striking when one considers that it has coincided with a rapidly rising *supply* of educated workers. The education premium declined somewhat in the late 1970s as newly graduated baby boomers flooded the labor market, but more recently the bonus skilled workers command has continued to increase even in the face of climbing levels of educational attainment.[24] In 1980, 11.5 percent of working men had bachelor's degrees, and an additional 9.8 percent had postgraduate education of some kind. By 1996, the fraction of male workers with bachelor's degrees had almost doubled, as older workers with limited schooling retired and were replaced by more-educated younger workers, while the proportion of postgraduate workers had grown by nearly a third.[25] Normally one would expect so sharp an expansion in the supply of skilled workers to batter down the education premium; when employers have a deeper reservoir from which to draw their skilled workers they needn't pay so dearly to staff up with the right kind of labor. Yet the economy's appetite for workers with advanced skills has become so intense that even the booming supply of high-level labor has failed to narrow the education premium. At *some* point, no doubt, increases in the fraction of skilled workers would begin to overwhelm the demand for skills, but we seem to be very far from that point today. In sum, "skill-biased" technological change—that is, change that alters the relative return to worker education and training—is very likely the largest single cause of growing wage dispersion, and a major contributor to family income inequality.[26]

Wage and Workplace Laws and Institutions

However much pressure global markets and technological change exert on the earnings distribution, this pressure is channeled by laws, regulations, and institutional structures. An increase in apparel imports, an influx of illegal immigrants, or the diffusion of automated teller machines will have one set of consequences if minimum wage laws put a floor under hourly pay, for example, and another set of consequences if wages are allowed to fall to whatever level the new market conditions dictate. The ultimate effect on employment and wages of new telecommunications technologies, or expert systems for bookkeeping, or a merger between a U.S. airline and a European airline, will depend in part on whether affected employees are covered by union contracts; whether they have legal protection against summary layoffs; and whether (by law, or custom, or contract) they have a voice in corporate decision-making.

The term "labor-market institutions" serves as a conventional shorthand for the portfolio of factors constraining the range of outcomes that the market for labor would otherwise produce. Pure logic does not require such factors to push the economy toward greater equality, to be sure. If labor markets, left alone, would generate a relatively flat income distribution, then institutional interventions could actually widen economic disparities. For example, if wages started out uniform throughout an economy and half of the workers

suddenly formed exclusive unions, wages would rise for the organized half of the workforce at the expense of the unorganized half,
spoiling the egalitarian idyll. Such a world is very far from our own,
however, and in practice studies generally find that weak American
labor-market institutions—whether institutional peculiarities distin-
guishing the United States from other advanced countries, or changes
over time within this country—help to explain the inequality story.

What economic historian Claudia Goldin has termed the "great
compression" in the American wage distribution in the middle third
of this century was partly caused by the wartime surge in labor
demand—itself perhaps a product of policy, if one stretches the
definition—but also by the flurry of New Deal policy innovations.
The Fair Labor Standards Act of 1938 put a meaningful federal floor
under wages, and within a decade of the passage of the National
Labor Relations Act the unionization rate had risen from 12 to 35
percent.[27] The more recent evolution of "institutional" factors, however, has been in the opposite direction. As recently as 1981 the minimum wage was 43 percent of the average wage in manufacturing,
but it fell to 31 percent in 1990, exerting progressively less influence over labor-market outcomes. The fraction of the workforce
belonging to labor unions fell slowly through the early postwar
years—29 percent in 1960, 25 percent in 1979—then plummeted to
below 15 percent (and to only 10 percent for private-sector workers)
by 1996.[28]

As with any interventions into complex markets, determining
the effects of labor-market policies and institutions tends to be both
methodologically challenging and ideologically controversial.
Minimum-wage laws may raise some workers' pay while pricing others out of the workforce; unions may benefit their members at the
expense of uncovered workers. On balance, however, the weakening
of such institutions in the United States has almost certainly contributed to rising inequality. Unions tend to narrow pay differentials
significantly, even controlling for the tendency of unionized work-
places to attract different kinds of workers than nonunionized ones,[29]
and around 10 to around 20 percent of the growth in wage inequality appears attributable to declining unionization.[30] The decline in
the value of the minimum wage—relative to the overall price level,
and relative to the rewards the market accords higher-paid workers—
has probably been the cause of around a tenth of the increase in wage

dispersal overall, and may have been a much larger factor for female workers.

A more diffuse sort of evidence about the importance of labor-market institutions comes from comparing nations like Britain, Canada, and the United States (where labor markets are relatively unconstrained by either law or custom) with countries like Germany, France, and Sweden that enforce high minimum wages, encourage labor organization, or guarantee employees a voice in management. Nations with stronger institutional constraints on labor markets tend to have substantially less wage dispersion and a much narrower distribution of family income.[31] And an even broader explanation looks beyond particular economic institutions to some pervasive aspects of American culture that acquiesce in economic disparities—among a firm's best- and worst-paid employees, for example—wider than what other advanced countries find tolerable.[32]

WHY DOES INEQUALITY MATTER?

Growing economic inequality is a fact; only the most tortured sorts of arguments, which few any longer even attempt to advance, can cast doubt on the trend. But whether inequality is a *problem* invites a subtler type of debate. Some observers sincerely reject inequality as a legitimate policy issue. All but the very poorest Americans, after all, are rich beyond the dreams of most who live, or have ever lived, on Earth. Why spoil this national triumph with quibbles that some Americans happen to be richer than others? One could argue that we should simply celebrate the affluents' good fortune, follow their example, and shun the sour politics of envy. Others stress that the real issue isn't *unequal* income growth but *inadequate* income growth: The problem isn't that a happy minority of Americans have escaped the slowdown of recent decades, but that a majority has succumbed to it. Do what it takes to boost productivity, runs the prescription inspired by this diagnosis, and don't get sidetracked by sterile concerns about distribution.

Almost anyone will agree that there are worse things than inequality, especially if nobody (or nearly nobody) lies starving and naked in the gutter. As social problems go, our unbalanced bounty is a nice one to have. The last great reduction in American inequality coincided with a searing depression and a genocidal world war. If we somehow were to discover that the only way to reverse the recent growth in inequality would be to go through *that* again, any sane person would rather live with an economically divided society. But this is not the choice before us, and there is much to be said in favor of serious efforts to reverse recent trends and bring American income distribution in the next generation closer to the pattern of a generation ago.

Start with the tidiest (if not necessarily the most compelling) case against excessive inequality. A building block of economic theory is the notion of "declining marginal utility of income." If people have the wit to spend their money first on what makes them happiest, they will devote the first $10,000 to the goods and services that yield the greatest increase in their welfare. The next $10,000 will go to somewhat less urgent purposes, and so on until the money runs out, with each slice of purchasing power bringing a smaller gain in welfare than the one before. Extending this logic, a given $10,000 might be expected to deliver more happiness to a family whose income would otherwise be $30,000 than to a family that already has $300,000 to spend. This is the core of the theoretical economic case for why a narrower income distribution is preferable (all else being equal) to a wider one. But the claim that every new increment of income buys a progressively smaller gain in happiness (while doubtless consistent with most people's experience and intuition) is unproven and, indeed, unprovable. And increasing economic growth overall—which some claim is much harder to pull off if high inequality is ruled out of bounds—is a comparably effective and perhaps less divisive way to get more money into the hands of the family with $30,000. So economic theory is a weaker voice than it might seem to be on the desirability of a more equal income distribution, and other perspectives— psychological, political, philosophical, even religious—quite legitimately come into play.

Some Americans (including me) believe that the economic disparities the country now displays, let alone those that would result from playing out recent trends for another generation or so, undermine community and enfeeble our culture. But others disagree, and I do not expect to make much headway here on grand issues of distributive justice. Instead I will note a few reasons for preferring less to more inequality that don't hinge on strenuous philosophical arguments, and that might be embraced even by those in the most fortunate fifth of the income distribution—a category that probably includes many readers of this essay. (If your 1996 family income exceeded $75,000, you were in the top fifth.)

Contemporary extremes in income disparities may contribute to perverse excesses of consumerism as the spending habits of the affluent, vividly displayed in the mass media, ratchet up the standard to which other Americans aspire. This could help explain both the paradox of a bankruptcy epidemic in boom times and the nation's lamentably low savings rate; many among the less-affluent majority may be spending beyond their means to keep up with the top 5 percent.[33]

Economic inequality can complicate collective decisions and render our politics more frustrating and fractious. The wider the disparities in Americans' economic circumstances, the more their policy priorities are likely to diverge, and the harder it becomes to stake out common ground. Fortunate families, for example, may be willing to make some sacrifices in the name of long-term goals like forestalling global warming or preserving first-growth forests, while the less affluent (even if they care just as much about the underlying goals) may perceive the sacrifices as excessive. Parks and libraries may deteriorate as the more fortunate find well-maintained public spaces superfluous, and the less fortunate find them unaffordable luxuries. Tough crime control measures that seem urgent to inner-city residents may strike those sheltered in upper-income suburbs as unduly draconian. The well-off may support free trade, while the less fortunate find it threatening. (Trade economists are all but unanimous that the United States is admirably positioned to benefit from open markets, and form a chorus of exasperated commentary on the narrow approval of NAFTA in 1994 and the rejection three years later of "fast track" authority for negotiating new trade agreements. The skewed distribution of trade's risks and gains within a highly unequal economy helps to explain this puzzling political result.)

Practical politics is a matter of reconciling interests in conflict, of course, but the greater the economic distances dividing the electorate the harder it becomes to cobble together a public agenda that most citizens can live with. At least a little (and perhaps a lot) of the growing edginess in our politics and Americans' exasperation with government are probably attributable to diverging priorities due to income disparities.

High levels of inequality can make even the affluent uneasy. As the rungs on the economic ladder grow farther apart, even the most fortunate may feel insecure as the stakes of bad luck or misjudgment escalate. Relatedly, balancing work with family and community becomes trickier as a rising price must be paid for focusing less single-mindedly on one's career. Consider a high-earning family contemplating a reallocation of priorities—the wife working half-time to meet young children returning from school or to launch a community group; the husband stepping off the fast track to free up evenings for volunteer work or to help the kids with their homework—that would lower their income from the average of the top twentieth to the average of the top fifth. In 1980, this would have entailed an income loss of 29 percent. By 1996, the sacrifice had risen to 42 percent. Taking more modest vacations or replacing the car in six years instead of two may seem a price worth paying for civic engagement or work-family balance; moving to a cheaper town may not. Laments about overwork, neglected families, and the lack of time for volunteer activities could have a good deal to do with the scale of the sacrifice a growingly unequal economy imposes on those who settle for something other than first place in the workplace marathon.

A closely related feature of contemporary life is the chilly careerism often noted among today's middle-class youth. Every year since the mid-1960s, the Higher Education Research Institute has surveyed a large sample of college freshmen to track attitudes and aspirations among students. One potential goal of higher education—"to be very well off financially"—has soared in importance over the past quarter-century while another—"to develop a meaningful philosophy of life"—has plummeted. In 1968, 41 percent of freshmen saw financial security as an "essential" goal of education, compared to 75 percent of their counterparts in 1997. A "meaningful philosophy of life" was an essential goal for 83 percent of the 1968 freshmen, and 41 percent of the 1997 freshmen. Conventional interpretations of this and similar cultural gauges point with alarm to the characteristic (and amply reinforced) cynicism of modern youth, or bemoan the shallowness and materialism of generations weaned on television.[34] But the widening income spectrum may explain as much as cultural evolution.

College confronts young people with some basic choices over priorities. Students can stress the practical potential of a college education—cultivating grade-point averages; pursuing programs leading to business, law, or medical degrees; minimizing the risks and distractions of political engagement, unfamiliar courses, and extracurricular activities. Or they can invest the college years less pragmatically by sampling a wide range of courses and by allocating some of their time and energy to volunteerism, politics, travel, late-night talks, and other amenities of campus life that have little to do with future earning power. If students in 1997 made different choices from students in 1968, it may be that the kids have changed[35]—or it may be that the consequences of their choices, and the context in which they choose, have changed.[36]

It would be preposterous to suggest that the freshmen of 1968 behaved as they did out of economic rationality, calculating and judging acceptable the expected loss of future income incurred by reading Proust or Popper instead of organic chemistry. But the penalty for letting pragmatism lapse during the college years looked smaller to them than it does to their children's generation. As gaps widen between those who are "very well off financially," and those lower down in the distribution, it becomes more understandable, perhaps, why today's freshmen think twice about indulging in the less practical opportunities campus life presents. Draining from the college years the aura of risk and romance that once defined them may not be a particularly weighty consequence of widening inequality, but it could turn out to be a small, sad footnote to the larger story.

More pervasively, economic disparities contribute to the erosion of community, the fading of civility, and the cultural fragmentation that are widely lamented hallmarks of contemporary American life. No less startling an authority than Gertrude Stein, early in this century, celebrated America's middle class as "the one thing always healthy, human, vital and from which has always sprung the best the world can know."[37] As that middle-class heritage ebbs, and Americans become isolated from one another by widening economic divisions, the consequences may be broader and more profound than we can yet predict. In short, there are some good arguments for even the winners of the income sweepstakes to prefer a more forgiving game. And the losers, of course, have a still longer list of reasons to regret rising inequality.[38]

3

GOVERNMENT'S SHIFT TOWARD THE STATES

Federal-state tension is engineered into America's political genes, and dates from our country's earliest days. The manifest failure of the Articles of Confederation—America's first draft at nationhood—forced patriots to regroup after only a few years of independence for an effort to "form a more perfect Union." The core dilemma the Framers faced was that weak government is prone to degenerate into muddle or mob rule, while strong government tends to harden into tyranny. The key to their solution was to craft a government that would be quite strong, in total, but to *divide* that strength along two dimensions. The first dimension of division would be *within* the national government; powers were separated among distinct legislative, judicial, and executive branches. The second dimension involved the seeming paradox of sharing sovereignty between the central government and the individual states. Such a scheme offered hope for merging the virtues of small and large polities, while dodging the evils of each. Yet while the Framers concurred on the basic design, they differed fiercely on matters of degree and on crucial details. Some merely intended somewhat stronger ties among essentially separate entities. Others envisaged a single new nation that would supersede the existing states. The outcome of this debate, encoded in the

Constitution, fell between these two poles—but precisely *where* it fell has been hotly debated throughout our history.

After the overture of the Revolution, the early scenes of American history seemed to highlight state sovereignty, as the once-formidable Federalists faded. But in practice, national integration was a steady theme of America's first decades. The Jefferson administration, in spite of the president's declared aversion to central authority, deployed federal resources to speed westward expansion by subsidizing infrastructure and education.[1] John Marshall, who played an enormous role in defining the Supreme Court's place in the American system, had been a soldier in the Revolutionary War and believed that "state particularism and national weakness were as deadly as British musket fire."[2] Ambiguities were settled in favor of national unity by the Supreme Court's key decisions in *McCulloch* v. *Maryland* (1816) and *Gibbons* v. *Ogden* (1824).[3]

As the nineteenth century reached its midpoint, American federalism neared its most searing test. Pressures accumulated along the fault line of slavery. A growing fraction of Americans considered the institution repugnant. Their willingness to tolerate its practice elsewhere in the name of state discretion eroded. The slave states held that the principles enshrined in the Tenth Amendment left decisions about slavery to the states alone. As absolutes collided, the sentiment of union crumbled. The South asserted what it declared to be the ultimate right of sovereign states—the right to opt out. State authority, Lincoln countered, did not go so far. The matter was settled by the most traumatic passage in American history. The Civil War and Reconstruction propelled authority toward the federal government.[4] Prosecuting the war had itself accelerated the growth of Washington's power, and preserving the union by force of arms dramatized the abstraction of American nationhood.

Another turning point in America's endless argument over federal-state balance came with the New Deal. An unprecedented degree of federal activism on the economy meant an unprecedented concentration of authority.[5] The massive national mobilization of the Second World War (and the cold war that followed) was a further force for centralization. And the prosperity of the first postwar decades seemed to affirm the wisdom of a strong federal hand at the economic tiller. Events beyond the economic realm, meanwhile, reinforced the shift toward Washington. As the struggle for civil rights escalated, "states' rights" became an unsavory code phrase, and recalcitrant Southern states faced vigorous assertions of federal authority. By the 1970s, the federal government had gained a role in virtually every public function, in virtually every state.

But Washington's dominance was nearing its high-water mark. The term "new federalism" surfaced at least a century ago, but only since the late 1960s has it been a staple of American political discourse. Two modern Republican presidents, Nixon and Reagan, both launched major restructurings flying the "New Federalism" banner, although they used the same words to mean quite different things. Congressional Republicans of the mid-1990s, meanwhile, employed the term for their own distinctive purposes.

The basic idea of Nixon's variant of New Federalism was to shift from the Great Society's "categorical" grants, which cast state and local governments as Washington's agents or subcontractors, to spending *funded* by the federal government but *controlled* at lower levels—essentially a step toward the fiscal model prevailing in other modern federations where a substantial fraction of the revenue raised centrally is passed on to regional governments with few strings attached.[6] General revenue sharing surged from less than $500 million in 1970 to over $8.6 billion in 1980.[7]

Ronald Reagan's New Federalism, paradoxically, was at once more narrowly pragmatic than Nixon's and a far more aggressive repudiation of the turn that American history had taken. It was pragmatic in its concern for shielding the federal fisc. Instead of providing resources while ceding control, Reagan sought to renounce the federal government's responsibilities over large areas of policy. It was profound, indeed radical, in its ambition of undoing several stages of national consolidation. The 1981 Omnibus Budget Reconciliation Act that set the tone for the Reagan era folded roughly one-tenth of the 534 existing categorical programs into nine block grants.[8] Overall transfers from Washington to states and cities, which had accounted for about 3.5 percent of the overall economy in the mid-1970s, retreated under Reagan and Bush.

The early years of the first Clinton administration were characterized by ambivalence on the federal-state balance; most of the initiatives that would have decisively engaged the issue—health care and job-training reform, for example—failed to survive the passage to legislation. Bill Clinton had made his reputation as an innovative governor, and had considerable sympathy with the view from the states. The administration's agenda for federalism, in any case, became considerably less determinative with the 1994 congressional elections. The 104th Congress included seventeen former governors and thirty-eight former state representatives among the one hundred senators, and nearly half of the members of the House had previously served as state legislators, while the number of Republican governors leaped from nineteen to thirty-one in a single year.[9]

As advocates of state primacy found their voice, the nationalist side of the argument was strangely muted. Washington acquiesced in the ascendancy of the states, and not only because of Republican dominance of both Congress and the statehouses. President Clinton, from what precise mix of conviction and stratagem it is difficult to say, proved broadly agreeable to letting the states take the lead, endorsing what he termed an "inexorable move to push more basic jobs of the public sector back to the state level."[10] The 1996 Democratic platform featured the taunt that "Republicans talked about shifting power back to states and communities—Democrats are doing it."[11]

So with little coherent counterforce from any political quarter, the tide is flowing away from Washington and toward the states by three critical gauges of governmental power—legitimacy, authority, and resources.

Legitimacy

State governments have been spared the worst effects of Americans' disenchantment with the public sector. Popular preference for lower-level governments may seem like the natural order of things, but it was not always so. Half a century ago, a Gallup poll found that 56 percent of Americans favored concentrating power in the federal government, while 44 percent favored state authority. Forty-one percent of respondents in a 1939 Roper poll felt the federal government was "most honest and efficient in performing its own special duties." The states came in last (at 12 percent) in this New Deal-era poll, with 17 percent awarding their confidence to local governments.[12]

Contemporary opinion surveys, by contrast, show limited confidence in the federal government and (at least in relative terms) rising state legitimacy. Asked which level of government was "more likely to administer social programs efficiently," 20 percent of the Americans surveyed in 1995 by Gallup opted for Washington, while 74 percent favored the states.[13] A Hart and Teeter poll conducted in 1995 for the Council for Excellence in Government found 64 percent favoring the concentration of public power at the state level versus 26 percent at the federal level. Seventy-five percent favored giving states more responsibility for programs currently run by the federal government. In no policy area did a majority endorse giving Washington the lead.[14] Some striking findings emerge from a bellwether poll conducted in 1995 for the *Washington Post*, the Kaiser Family Foundation, and Harvard University. By a margin of 61 to 24 percent, respondents trusted their state governments over the federal government to "do a better job of running things."[15]

Authority

Welfare reform is the most vivid recent example of authority flowing to lower levels of government. National legislation passed and signed in 1996 repudiates a sixty-year tradition of federal responsibility for antipoverty policies. An intricate and little loved federal-state system that previously guaranteed some level of assistance to poor families with children has been replaced by substantially autonomous state programs. The national role is restricted to offering states block grants (at whatever level Congress deems appropriate) with few strings attached, beyond an imperative of austerity.

Other examples suggest the breadth of the trend. Legislation championed in 1995 by both the Republican Congress and the Clinton administration sheltered states from "unfunded mandates," by which Congress endorsed popular goals while leaving to other governments the obligation to deliver on the promises. The law requires Congress to identify and estimate the size of any burdens imposed on states and cities by new legislation, and either come up with a way to pay for the burden or explain explicitly why it should not.[16] Barriers to the imposition of unfunded mandates, while a step toward more accountable government, amplify the influence of state authority in any conflict of priorities. Within specific policy areas, legislation passed in the 1990s has expanded state discretion over transportation spending, drinking water standards, and highway safety.

The pattern is by no means unmixed; over the same period, there have been moves to lengthen the list of federal crimes and to *restrict* state autonomy on the legal drinking age and product liability, among other issues. (The White House and the governors have been wrangling over which level of government—federal or state—gets to decide how many monthly doses of Viagra Medicaid should allow citizens afflicted by both impotence and indigence.)[17] But while amended by episodes of expediency and inconsistency on the part of policy-makers, the general trend remains toward the states.

Resources

By the simplest possible measure—total spending as a share of the economy—Washington has begun to retreat from its postwar peak of over 22 percent in the 1980s to an average of 21.5 percent for 1990 through 1997 (and barely 20 percent for 1997). But self-funded state and local spending—even excluding the substantial fraction of subnational spending that is covered by federal grants—has grown from around 5 percent of the economy in the 1950s, to around 6.5 percent in the 1960s, then around 8 percent in the 1970s and 1980s, to an average of 9.4 percent so far in the 1990s.[18]

Comparing overall national and subnational public spending actually obscures the states' relative importance in the average American's experience of what the public sector does. In part this is because around one-fifth of subnational government activities are sustained by intergovernmental grants and hence recorded in the accounts as "federal" spending, even though the actual operations are conducted by states and localities. Moreover, much of the federal budget is devoted to defense and international affairs or to "check-writing" functions—paying interest on the debt or issuing grants—rather than to direct governmental operations. Most commentary on the composition of American public spending concentrates, accurately enough, on the fall in defense spending and the rise in entitlements and other transfers over recent decades. Yet a subtler trend may turn out to be equally important—the growing fiscal weight of state and local government *within* the domestic sphere.

Figure 3.1 looks at broad patterns of American public spending over the postwar decades, separating the large "federal" category into four broad components: defense and international, debt interest, grants (which includes Social Security, Medicare, and intergovernmental transfers), and the residual category of "everything else" the federal government does. As defense and international spending plummeted from over 11 percent of the economy in the 1950s to an average of 4.5 percent in the 1990s, transfer spending expanded to more than fill the gap, from under 4 percent to nearly 12 percent. And as the federal debt exploded in the 1980s, interest payments soared from the prevailing postwar levels of around 1.25 percent of GDP to reach an average of 2.3 percent between 1990 and 1997. Federal spending on everything other than defense, transfers, and interest averaged 3.6 percent of the economy in the 1970s, but has dropped back to an average of 2.2 percent through the 1990s, and was only 1.5 percent in 1997. Meanwhile, self-funded state and local spending has continued to climb. One way to summarize the shift

FIGURE 3.1 PUBLIC SPENDING AS SHARES OF GDP, 1950–97

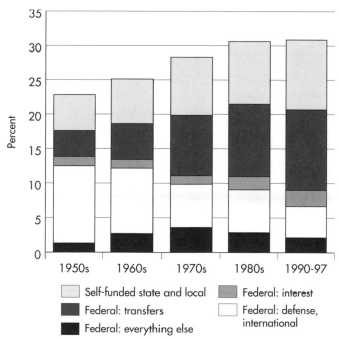

Source: U.S. Office of Management and Budget, *Budget of the United States Government Fiscal Year 1999* (Washington, D.C.: U.S. Government Printing Office, 1997), Historical Table 15.5 (www.access.gpo/su_docs/ budget99/ hist15.5_wk1).

toward the states in domestic public spending is this: In the late 1970s, total state and local spending was a little less than twice as large as total federal domestic spending apart from transfers and interest. In the late 1990s, it's about seven times as large. So within what most Americans think of as "the government," states and cities occupy a large and growing share of the terrain.[19]

The same tide away from Washington can be discerned in the balance of *human* resources. Federal civilian employment was around 3 million from the mid-1980s to the mid-1990s, but fell to about 2.7 million in 1997 and is slated to drop further. As a share of the U.S. population, the federal civilian payroll is now barely one percent. (The uniformed military payroll has dropped even more precipitously, from something approaching 2 percent of the population in the Vietnam era to around half a percent today.) But state and local employment has reached nearly 17 million—well over 6 percent of the population, and more than half again as large, on a per-capita basis, as it had been in the 1960s. The rising *quality* of state government intensifies the quantitative shift. There has been a quiet, decades-long migration of talent toward state capitals. Twenty or thirty years ago state politics was decidedly minor-league; today, the caliber of state officials frequently exceeds the federal standard.

The conventional image of enfeebled states prostrate before the federal behemoth, in short, is somewhere between oversimplified and preposterous. Yet while the balance has already been shifting toward the states, the call for *further* decentralization enjoys something as close to consensus as American politics often sees. Proponents predict greater efficiency, stepped-up innovation, and even a softening of antigovernment sentiments as power moves closer to the people. Nor, to be sure, are such claims groundless. The conceptual case for leaving the lead to the states has an undeniable appeal. Yet the tilt toward state-based government promises perhaps more far-reaching consequences than the noisier debate over the federal budget. The fragmentation of America's public sector may well dim our prospects for narrowing economic disparities and preserving a middle-class society.

4

DEVOLUTION AND INEQUALITY

Some manifestations of America's shift toward the states—which is commonly, if not quite accurately, described as "devolution"[1]—have rather little to do with economic inequality. Whether federal or state politicians set speed limits in Utah; whether state or federal rules constrain purchases of pistols in New York; whether federal or state laws determine the outcome of defective-product claims in Minnesota—have only indirect, and mostly minor, implications for whether family incomes will once again grow together or will continue to diverge.

Many of the leading causes of economic inequality likewise have little to do with the locus of public authority or the degree of centralization in taxing and spending. Trade and immigration policies are overwhelmingly federal, and in the absence of radical constitutional revision will remain so. The integration of global markets, in any case, follows no government's script. Similarly, the rise in divorce and single parenthood and the surge of women into the workforce have not been driven by rearrangements of governmental responsibility and will not be altered to any great degree by shifts in the federal balance. It is certainly possible to tell stories linking devolution with global integration or changes in family structure, but for the most part such stories will be either unconvincing or peripheral to the larger phenomenon of economic inequality.

**FIGURE 4.1 MID-1990s RATIO OF TOP-QUINTILE
TO BOTTOM-QUINTILE FAMILY INCOME**

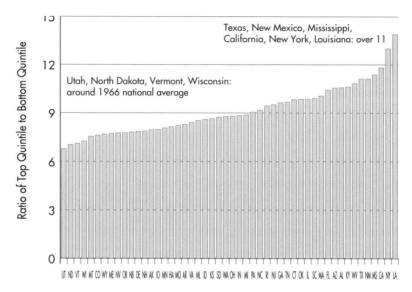

Source: Calculated from Current Population Survey state-level data compiled by Jon Haveman of Purdue University and the Council of Economic Advisors and supplied to the author.

Yet there is reason to suspect that state policy matters. One hint comes from the fact that the states vary quite a lot in the degree of economic inequality they display. Figure 4.1 ranks the states, from least to most unequal, by the ratio of income for the top fifth of families to income for the bottom fifth in the mid-1990s. Inequality differs as much among the states, at a single point in time, as it has for the nation as a whole over the past thirty years. The states with the least inequality, like Utah, North Dakota, Vermont, and Wisconsin, had mid-1990s income distributions resembling the national average for 1966, with the most affluent fifth earning about seven times as much as the least affluent. Mid-range states, like Indiana, Pennsylvania, North Carolina and Michigan, looked like the national average had a decade earlier, as the surge of inequality was beginning to gather force, with top-quintile families earning around nine times as much as those at the bottom. And a set of "vanguard" states—Texas, New Mexico, Mississippi, California, New York, and Louisiana—already exceeded the level of inequality that the nation as a whole would not attain until late in the decade.[2] Not all these differences are rooted in policy, to be sure, but even if state policy choices—rather than demographics, culture, industrial structure, or natural endowments—explain only a fraction of the variation, the range is sufficiently great that even a partial account would warrant considerable interest.

WHAT'S DIFFERENT ABOUT STATE-LEVEL DECISIONS?

To appreciate the potential links between devolution and inequality, consider some generic reasons to expect that policies will differ systematically when decisions are made state by state. Many features of public life hold at any level of government—the eternal tension between self and community, the challenge of reconciling wants in conflict, the delicate architecture of political representation and governmental accountability. Whether the immediate forum is a town meeting, a state legislature, or the U.S. Congress, some fundamental things apply. But in certain crucial respects, decentralization makes a difference.[3] State-level policy debates may disregard, or exploit, consequences that fall beyond a state's boundaries. And interstate competition can render the dynamics of state-level deliberations quite different from national debates.

An extensive academic literature, developed mostly by economists but also by political scientists, deals with competition among governments. This tradition generally celebrates competitive decentralization as a spur to public-sector accountability, invoking the private market ideal of efficiency through competition as a metaphor for improving the public sector. The literature on intergovernmental competition recognizes that constituents vary in their preferences, their endowments, and the priorities they place on alternative public policies. (Indeed, it is such differences that make competition among heterogeneous governments so intellectually attractive to economists; if preferences and endowment were identical there would be less pay-off from diversity.) But two of the most important dimensions along which constituents differ are too little stressed: First, in their relative *mobility*, and second, in their relative *desirability* as constituents, from the perspective of officials in competing states.

Suppose for the moment that individuals and institutions were either entirely mobile, or entirely immobile, instead of the minutely varied range we actually see. Suppose, too, that potential constituents could be categorized as either desirable to state policy-makers (by whatever criteria the officials hold dear) or flatly undesirable. Then competitive state policy-makers' generic strategies could be summarized along the lines of Table 4.1.

To the extent competition for constituents is the primary force behind officials' deliberations—an important qualification—then policies will be crafted to *attract* individuals and institutions that are both desirable and mobile (productive citizens with no special needs, for example, or high-growth businesses). Competition-minded officials would find it rational to *exploit* constituents that are desirable but *not* mobile (corporations with immovable assets, for example). They would seek to *repel* mobile, undesirable constituents (such as low-paying or highly polluting industries, or individuals prone to crime or dependency). And the basic stance toward undesirable, immobile individuals and institutions would be neglect. The real world is infinitely more complex than this tidy framework suggests, to be sure. Pure cases are seldom seen, and internal politics is an ever-present counterpoint to interstate competition. But competitive strategizing, and the related incentive for one state's officials to ignore or to exploit the out-of-state consequences of their decisions, renders state-level decision-making different from collective choices made at the national level, and the implications can be profound. The rest of this essay examines four specific policy areas where fragmented policy-making is a plausible contributing or aggravating factor to American economic inequality: tax structure, antipoverty policy, labor policy, and education finance.

TABLE 4.1 CONSTITUENTS' CHARACTERISTICS AND COMPETITIVE STATE STRATEGIES

	MOBILE	IMMOBILE
DESIRABLE	attract	exploit
UNDESIRABLE	repel	neglect

5

TAX STRUCTURE

Tax structure has an important but indirect connection to economic inequality. In principle, to be sure, the link could be absolutely central. One could imagine an aggressively redistributive tax system that would cancel out any degree of economic inequality that the market could generate, by levying high taxes on those who fare well in the earnings race and paying out negative "taxes" to those who fare badly. But explicit redistribution of this sort has never been a major factor in the United States, and probably never will be. The Earned Income Tax Credit, the most important contemporary example, has significant but circumscribed impacts and is a minor element in the big fiscal picture. Aside from any deleterious effects such wholesale redistribution might have on economic efficiency, it simply violates most Americans' sense of fairness.

Yet even if tax policy is unlikely to overturn disparities in pretax income, it could far more realistically be structured to lessen their sting. A progressive tax structure—which claims a smaller fraction of income at lower levels of income and a larger fraction at higher levels—tilts the burden of common responsibilities away from those with more meager means and thus cushions the impact of inequality. So as income gaps widen, the stakes for tax progressivity grow.

The overall structure of taxation remains reasonably progressive in the United States, mostly because the federal income tax forms a large (if shrinking) fraction of total taxation. But in addition to the much-discussed rise in the share of regressive federal payroll taxes in the overall tax burden, shifts toward (and shifts within) subnational taxation imperil this progressivity. Total state and local tax revenues have gone from an average of 8.5 percent of the gross domestic product in the 1960s to an average of 10.7 percent so far in the 1990s, and the subnational share of government revenues has gone from 33 percent to 37 percent.[1] If anything approximating current budget plans actually forms Washington's fiscal script for the near future, we will likely see a further shift toward subnational taxation. The point, from the perspective of progressivity, is that federal and state budgets rest on very different revenue foundations.

Figure 5.1 shows the sources of federal receipts for fiscal year 1997. Social Security and related contributions have reached over a third of federal revenues, and while the *spending* side of Social Security is progressive, the *taxing* side is decidedly not. But the largest single category of federal revenues, accounting for nearly half of the total, is the personal income tax. The federal income tax is sharply progressive; early 1980s moves toward regressivity have been mostly undone by subsequent legislation. Treasury Department data from around 170 million returns filed in 1994 and 1995 show that filers with annual income of under $10,000 paid an average of about 4 percent of their incomes in taxes; those with incomes between $30,000 and $50,000 paid about 10 percent; those with incomes between $100,000 and $200,000 paid around 18 percent; and those with incomes over $500,000 paid 30 percent or more.[2] Endless debates rage over who actually pays the corporate income tax—how the bill is finally shared out among stockholders, customers, and suppliers once all the adjustments ripple through the system—but this 12 percent slice of federal revenue is probably progressive as well. (It is hard to generalize about the 8 percent "other" category, but the slice is too small to matter much relative to the major categories. Gift and estate taxes are progressive, but are a trivial share of revenues. Customs duties are regressive, but also small.)

The state revenue picture is more complex and, on balance, far less progressive. About 23 percent of state revenues have nothing to do with state taxes or fees, but instead represent transfers from the federal government. Figure 5.2 shows the breakdown of the revenues states raise themselves. One factor worth noting is that regressive payroll

FIGURE 5.1 FEDERAL RECEIPTS, FISCAL YEAR 1997
TOTAL: $1,578 BILLION

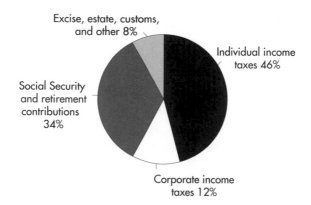

Source: Office of Management and Budget, *Budget of the United States Government Fiscal Year 1999* (Washington, D.C.: U.S. Government Printing Office, 1997), Summary Table 13 ("Receipts by Source: Summary") (www.access.gpo.gov/su_docs/budget99/summ_s13).

FIGURE 5.2 STATE REVENUES, FISCAL YEAR 1996
(EXCLUDING FEDERAL GRANTS) TOTAL: $775 BILLION

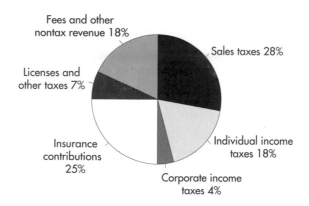

Source: U.S. Department of Commerce, Bureau of the Census, Governments Division, on-line data compilation, State Government Finance Data 1996, U.S. Total (www.census.gov/govs/state/96stus).

taxes are only around half as large a share of state revenues as are the comparable contributions at the federal level. But there the favorable comparison, in terms of progressivity at least, comes to an end. Corporate taxes form only one-third as large a fraction of state revenues as they do of federal revenues. Individual income taxes are also a much smaller revenue source at the state level—18 percent instead of 46 percent. Moreover, state income tax codes, as a group, are a great deal less progressive than the federal version. Six states had no personal income tax in 1994, while 34 states had either a flat rate for rich and poor alike or a top rate that kicked in at a level somewhere below $50,000 in annual income (and sometimes as low as $3,000). Only nine states had top brackets above $50,000, and only three increased tax rates as incomes passed $100,000.[3]

About half of all state revenues (aside from federal transfers) come from sales taxes, license taxes, service fees, and other levies that tend to weigh more heavily on lower-income citizens. More affluent families generally save more of their incomes—one of the nice things about rich people—and hence surrender a lower fraction to sales taxation. Many state tax codes, moreover, concentrate on physical goods, and spare many or all of the services that tend to figure more prominently in the consumption patterns of the better off. Even if upper-income taxpayers drive or drink more than their lower-income neighbors, they normally pay a smaller share of their earnings in gasoline and alcohol excise taxes. And the poor tend to spend more on tobacco taxes and lottery tickets not just relative to their incomes, but in absolute terms as well.

Why do revenue structures differ so dramatically between America's state and national levels? One reason is that the burden of state taxation tends to reflect relative mobility. Some individuals, and many institutions, are able to base their location decisions in part on tax rates. State officials understandably craft their tax codes to favor the more footloose and more desirable constituencies, at the expense of constituencies that are more rooted, or less worth courting, or both. Individuals differ in their responsiveness to state benefits and burdens, and in the strength of their social and economic attachment to a particular place. Those with tight family ties are more anchored than those without; the gregarious and the engaged are more anchored than the loners; those committed to a particular culture are more anchored than the cosmopolitan. Income seems to matter, too.

Adults with family incomes over $50,000 are about 25 percent more likely to move interstate than those with incomes in the $25,000 to $50,000 range.[4] The richest (adults with personal income exceeding $85,000) and the poorest (with income under $15,000) were *both* about 38 percent more likely to move across state borders between 1993 and 1994 than those earning between $30,000 and $85,000.[5]

Corporations and other institutions—which are usually unanchored by ties of culture and family—are even more promising objects for competitive state strategies. A leading theorist predicted many years ago that such strategies would tend to "produce either a generally low level of state-local tax effort or a state-local tax structure with strong regressive features."[6] The prediction has been amply realized. While it can be a complex matter to pinpoint just how progressive or regressive a tax code is, analysts display uncommon consensus that state taxes, as a class, are regressive.[7]

There are two implications, both disquieting for those concerned about inequality. First, the more the public sector's center of gravity shifts away from Washington, the more heavily will common burdens come to weigh on the less affluent. Tax structure will tend to amplify, rather than dampen, the growing inequality of market earnings. The second implication is more subtle: As states become more autonomous in major policy areas and more reliant on revenues they raise themselves, competitive pressures will work to render state tax codes still less progressive. This effect is likely to be gradual and halting. Internal politics favoring progressivity will sometimes trump interstate competition in particular tax debates. The tilt of the terrain at the state level, however, is decidedly unfavorable to progressive taxation.

Anxious to make themselves at least as hospitable to productive enterprise as neighboring states (and hopefully a bit more hospitable) states will refrain from burdening firms with corporate taxes, or with individual tax codes that fall heavily on the top workers firms need to recruit. These anxieties are by no means groundless, and one cannot fault state officials for structuring their taxes with an eye to competitive pressures.[8] On the national scale, the claim that reducing tax *rates* would actually increase tax *revenues* has been tested and found flatly wrong. But on the state level such effects are far more plausible, since the goal need not be to induce additional economic activity, but merely to move it around.

The booming American economy of the 1990s swelled state revenues, so that by the end of 1997 the states together held balances totaling over $28 billion, or 7.3 percent of general spending—the most comfortable fiscal cushion since the 1970s.[9] In response to this bonanza, 21 states salted away reserves for leaner times; 20 devoted some of their surpluses to special spending for education, local aid, economic development, or other priorities; 17 funded long-term capital projects; and 6 paid down debt. But the commonest response, pursued by 25 states, was to cut taxes. Indeed, 1997 marked the first time in decades that state taxes had been reduced for three years running, with legislatures enacting a total of nearly $10 billion in net reductions. There is nothing shocking about tax cuts in flush times, and (absent an implausibly rapid economic meltdown) any reasonable person would expect more of the same. Yet consider the *pattern* of these tax cuts.

The *more* heavily a class of taxes hits the lower reaches of the income distribution, the *less*, proportionately, it has been cut. Quarterly state data collected by the Census Bureau show that for the 1990–94 period (the baseline for the recent tax-cutting campaign) state sales taxes—which are the most regressive major category of state revenue—averaged 42.6 percent of total state taxes. But as legislatures pared taxes over the next three years, sales taxes came in for only 4.7 percent of the reductions. (See Figure 5.3.) Indeed, amid the flurry of state tax reductions the average state sales tax rate actually reached a record high, 5.13 percent, in 1996.[10] Corporate income taxes were only 6.6 percent of the 1990–94 baseline, but claimed a disproportionate 18 percent of the 1995–97 tax cuts. And (relatively) progressive personal income taxes, which totaled 32 percent of the baseline, accounted for 58 percent of the cuts.[11] Sometimes personal income taxes were cut in a way that increased progressivity, but often they were not.

Consider, for example, the three 1997 personal income cuts worth over $100 million. Connecticut lowered the rate on the first several thousand dollars of income, which benefits everyone but matters most to those of modest means. On the other hand, Iowa cut its bottom rate by 0.04 percentage points while lowering its *top* rate by 1.01 percentage points, and Arizona cut the marginal rate by 0.1 percent on incomes below $20,000, and by four times as much on incomes over $100,000.[12] In short, the more regressive the category

FIGURE 5.3 STATE TAX-CUT PRIORITIES, 1995–97

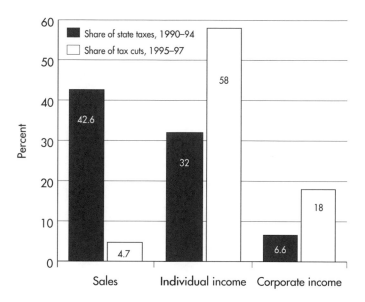

Sources: Early-1990s baseline calculated from data in U.S. Department of Commerce, Bureau of the Census, Governments Division, on-line compilation, Quarterly State and Local Tax Data, Table 2, "National Totals of State Tax Revenue, by Type of Tax" (www.census.gov/govs/qtax/qtx981); the 1995–97 tax-cut aggregates are from *State Tax Actions* (Louisville, KY: National Council of State Legislatures, 1995, 1996, and 1997 issues).

of state taxation, the lower its apparent priority for reduction in response to fiscal slack in the second half of the 1990s.

There is little reason to attribute this to some conspiracy, or to an animus against low earners on the part of state officials. States cannot be expected to allocate tax cuts (or, when the time comes, tax increases) in a way that repels the most successful workers or the firms that employ them. But the likely result will be a gradual evolution toward more regressive revenue structures in the states and, as states grow in importance, for the public sector as a whole. Since 1960, federal business taxes have been drifting downward as a share of the base on which the tax is levied, as (to a lesser extent) have federal individual income taxes. (See Figure 5.4, page 42.) Meanwhile, the burdens of the two most regressive grand categories of public revenue—payroll levies for Social Security and related programs, and state and local taxes—have more than doubled. As taxes

FIGURE 5.4 RELATIVE TAX PRESSURE INCREASE, 1960–95: BURDEN OF PAYROLL AND STATE AND LOCAL TAXES RISES WHILE FEDERAL PERSONAL AND BUSINESS TAX BURDENS DECLINE (INDEX: 1960=1.0)

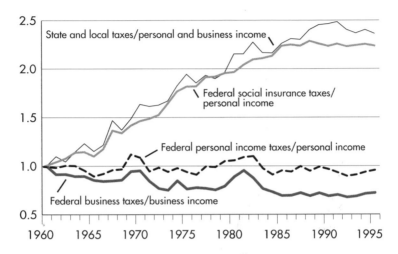

Sources: Data from Office of Management and Budget, *Budget of the United States Government Fiscal Year 1998* (Washington, D.C.: U.S. Government Printing Office, 1997), and Council of Economic Advisors, *Economic Report of the President 1997* (Washington, D.C.: U.S. Government Printing Office, 1997), various data sets and tables.

shift toward lower-income Americans, government becomes less of a counterweight to economic inequality. And to the extent taxation discourages enterprise, the regressive tilt in the country's tax structure will worsen inequality by depressing earnings among the less affluent.

6

ANTIPOVERTY POLICY

The emblem of government's shift toward the states—though a somewhat misleading one—is the Personal Responsibility Act of 1996, which renounced over a half-century of relatively centralized antipoverty policy and let states seek their own paths to welfare reform. If welfare devolution works as its advocates predict, it will help to reduce income inequality as states find ways to end dependency and launch former recipients onto trajectories of rising market earnings. If it works as its critics fear, it will deepen inequality as few former recipients find or keep good-paying jobs and the worst-off families see their incomes shrivel further. Welfare reform will one day provide powerful evidence on some fundamental debates over the proper federal balance in social policy.

But not yet. The legislation is too recent, the profusion of changes in state laws and organizations too fresh, and the economic history too limited to support much in the way of conclusions. Massive numbers of researchers have been deployed to examine what the states do with their newfound discretion and to measure the results, and in five or ten years we will have some basis for evaluation. At this stage, however, no honest person can reach any firm judgment about welfare reform. Yet the grand experiment is sufficiently central to this essay—even though antipoverty policy, like tax policy, concerns efforts to buffer rather than to reverse inequality in earnings—that a few words are required.

The early evidence is mixed, but there is certainly some cause for optimism among the proponents of decentralized antipoverty policy. The draconian austerity some critics predicted has not materialized. There have been scattered instances of harshness as welfare entitlements are abolished and term limits and work requirements enforced. But on the whole the states have shown considerable willingness to maintain antipoverty spending, and have displayed the kind of creativity and innovation expected of America's "laboratories of democracy."[1]

Yet the weight of historical experience, from Elizabethan England onward, offers sobering lessons about fragmented antipoverty policy. And there is a powerful conceptual case for the generalization that generosity, mobility, and decentralization form an unstable mix. Unless policies are centralized (or at least harmonized) or mobility is restricted, a syndrome of escalating austerity is easily triggered. Consider again the schematic of likely policy stances toward different groups, when interstate competition motivates state decisions. Perhaps the purest example of the southwestern quadrant of Table 4.1 (see page 34)—policies structured to repel constituents whom state officials, for whatever reason, consider undesirable, but who can move across state borders—is the frequently invoked prospect of becoming a "welfare magnet." Paul Peterson and Mark Rom have mapped out the dynamic in which state officials frame welfare policies while attempting to anticipate the reactions of needy individuals, officials in *other* states, their own taxpayers, and political rivals. Each state "fears to provide full services lest it become attractive to poor people. Since every state makes a similar calculation, redistribution levels do not reach the level that would probably be set by the national government."[2]

Warnings of a "race to the bottom" in antipoverty policy, however, have been (perhaps in a very precise sense of the term) premature. Benefit levels have not in fact converged in a common downward spiral; they varied as much among states in 1985 as they had in 1940, Peterson and Rom observe. (Indeed, President Clinton cited this range of variance in justifying his decision to sign the 1996 welfare reform legislation, dismissing the significance of dismounting the national system since "there's not really a national guarantee that amounts to much now."[3]) The poor, by and large, have not been roaming America in search of richer welfare benefits; the anchors of family and culture have generally outweighed the lure of more generous public assistance regimes. Prior to the mid-1990s, researchers found little evidence that differences in state welfare systems strongly affected migration patterns, and critics have sought to dismiss the "welfare magnet" scenario as empirically repudiated.[4] But even if the evidence were strongly against the hypothesis that generous benefits lure the poor—instead of merely ambiguous on the point—that would not be fatal to the argument that interstate competition will drive down benefits. This is so for two quite different reasons.

First, it matters considerably less whether poor people actually *do* move in search of higher benefits than whether voters and state officials *believe* they do, and there is ample evidence that governors have justified policy changes by reference to the welfare-magnet scenario.[5] Second, the 1996 welfare reform legislation radically changes the incentives of both needy citizens and state officials in ways that make an eventual "race for the bottom" far more probable than it ever was in the past.[6] Federal funding for needy families now comes in the form of block grants to the states, with no *individual* entitlement to assistance of any sort, and only whatever level of federal-to-state funding Congress chooses to provide for antipoverty programs. The initial block-grant budget, $16.4 billion, is based on state welfare caseloads from the early 1990s, and stays the same until 2002. Since the baseline was set during an era of relatively high demand for benefits, most states collect more in block grants than they would have under the old system—until inflation erodes the grants' real value, or until a recession hits, or unless they configure their policies in a way that increases the number of jobless beneficiaries. The big change in state officials' incentives comes from the fact that federal grants no longer rise and fall in line with state welfare spending. In the past an extra dollar spent on benefits, or a dollar saved through more stringent rules, had less (often much less) than a dollar's impact on the state budget. With block grants, every dime devoted to poor kids now means less for roads, schools, prisons, and economic development. There's a much bigger bottom-line payoff to cutting benefits (and a bigger penalty to keeping them high).

Beneficiaries, in turn, may well confront intensified incentives to migrate. In the past, the poor could count on *some* floor under benefit levels and eligibility rules whatever their home state. It is entirely possible that some states could opt for welfare regimes harsh enough to motivate at least some of the needy to search elsewhere. And that possibility—especially if it is exaggerated in the minds of state officials—sets the stage for competitive cuts in benefits. But, to be clear, it only sets the stage. Whether the players follow that particular script depends on the economic conditions and the political climate prevailing in the last year of this century and the early years of the next, and projections are inevitably speculative.

Many commentators dismiss predictions of a net decline in support for the poor. Mississippi governor Kirk Fordice rejects as a "disgusting elitist argument" the claim that state control will mean harsher treatment for the poor, countering that state officials are at least as compassionate as their federal counterparts, which may very well be true.[7] Mickey Kaus has written that governors "will be competing for the national prominence that will go not to the cruelest state, but to whoever figures out how best to get welfare recipients into the workforce."[8] Some states are indeed launched on such paths of reform. Other states may adopt these models, and the pioneers may continue to improve them through the end of the century in a "race to the top" unhindered by budgetary pressures or economic downturns.

Or the experiment might turn out otherwise. Imagine it's 2002, and Congress has whittled down the real value of the welfare block grants Washington sends to the states. A recession has swollen benefit claims, while unskilled jobs for former welfare recipients have evaporated. The evening news in Michigan, Wisconsin, or another pioneering state is full of stories about the ragged families streaming across the border for a chance at job training and the kind of support that boosts the odds of getting and keeping a decent job. In the statehouse briefing room, a grim-faced official takes the podium: "We don't want to be brutal. In a better world, we could continue our experiments with training, job-search help, and child care. But work-based reforms would be expensive even if we had only our own poor citizens to worry about. This state can't solve the problem of American poverty alone. It would be unfair to our kids if we go broke trying. The only responsible choice is to match what other states offer—no more, and maybe even a little less."

It is easy to picture a lot of decent politicians making that speech. It is somewhat harder to imagine states raising tax money (year after year, in good times and bad) to pay for costly welfare-to-work experiments, when the prize for success includes a higher share of the nation's poor.[9] While those who are skeptical about state-based antipoverty policy are well advised to hold their fire, it is not quite time to surrender. The devolution of antipoverty policy, I suspect, will eventually be seen as a mistake, if perhaps an inevitable mistake; the Gordian knot of the welfare status quo may have been beyond untangling by the mid-1990s, once the Clinton administration had failed to move its own version of work-based reform.

My guess—which at this stage can be no more than a guess— is that with the first serious recession, state-based welfare policy's built-in bias toward harshness will be revealed. As hard times swell the ranks of needy families while hobbling job-creation efforts; as welfare must compete with every other budget item for shrinking state funds; and as taxpayers and officials ponder the prospect (always riveting, and increasingly realistic) that anything but the sparest safety net will lure the poor from other states, antipoverty programs will spiral toward the furthest degree of austerity citizens' consciences will permit.[10] I would very much like to be proven wrong in this prediction. In any event, it will be years before serious revisions to the 1996 welfare reform reach the public agenda. Political realities at the federal level will preclude reversing course anytime soon. Nor is there yet any blueprint for how to achieve the humane, work-oriented welfare policy that virtually everyone endorses in principle. We have embarked upon a period of state-dominated antipoverty policy, and may as well make the best of it by harvesting every bit of evidence state experimentation produces. And we should hope that the country does not become too coarsened by what we will witness in the meantime.

7

LABOR POLICY

American labor policy is a complex amalgam of federal, state, and (to a considerably lesser extent) local laws and regulations. Compared to the norm in other industrialized countries, authority over workplace relations is highly fragmented in the United States. Federal law limits the length of the normal working week for many employees, mandates overtime pay for hours beyond that limit, bars many kinds of workplace discrimination, and requires employers to grant unpaid family and medical leave to certain classes of workers. Pay levels are constrained by national and (in some cases) state and even local minimum wages. Unemployment insurance is a joint enterprise, with federal and state governments intricately intertwined on matters of regulation, financing, and administration. Workers' compensation for on-the-job injuries is mostly the states' domain. And while federal law guarantees workers the right to organize and to bargain collectively, states have considerable control over the practical force of that guarantee within their borders.

Contemporary trends in labor policy, broadly defined, have almost certainly contributed to rising economic inequality. Arguments and evidence outlined earlier suggest that declining rates of labor organization, a relatively low minimum wage, and other features of American labor-market institutions are probably responsible for at least one-tenth and perhaps as much as one-third of the growth in wage inequality, and for a smaller but still significant share of the growth in family income inequality. The recent evolution of labor-market institutions has been caused in part by prevailing federal-level policy stances ranging between hostility and timidity toward labor interests, and in part by an individualistic American culture that tends to be deferential toward business prerogatives and wary about labor organization. But beyond these more obvious factors, it is highly probable that the fragmentation of labor-policy authority plays a role as well.

The basic logic goes like this: Transformations in industrial structure, along with improvements in transportation and communications technologies, are making businesses less anchored to any particular locale. Deregulation and global market integration, at the same time, heighten employers' sensitivities to the cost and tractability of their labor forces. Meanwhile, states are gaining more policy discretion, and their perennial preoccupation with economic development is becoming more intense as they must growingly fend for themselves. In such a setting, states may understandably become more solicitous of the priorities of mobile capital, and increasingly reluctant to risk repelling business by adopting or maintaining policies favoring labor.

Internal politics condition and constrain interstate competition, to be sure. If a state's political culture is hospitable toward labor interests, competitive considerations will dampen labor-friendly political impulses but may not extinguish them. If a state's political culture favors management interests, conversely, competitive imperatives may be superfluous. But so long as capital's mobility exceeds that of workers, decentralized labor policy coupled with interstate competition for investment will tend to mold state policy regimes that render workers cheap and compliant, instead of expensive and demanding. Under many conditions—including those that broadly prevail in the modern American economy—this syndrome would be expected to amplify other forces increasing economic inequality. Some specific areas of labor policy offer hints of whether and to what extent this syndrome actually occurs.

Minimum Wages

Minimum wage laws set a floor under hourly pay, essentially lopping off the low end of the wage distribution that would be generated by an unconstrained labor market. Their net impact on economic inequality depends on the balance between wage increases and employment reductions induced by this intervention, and on the circumstances of the workers affected. If minimum wage laws' main effect were to encourage employers to hire suburban teenagers instead of urban single mothers, such laws could *increase* family income inequality. If the main effect is to lead low-wage employers to pay somewhat more to something approaching the same number (and the same kind) of workers who would have been hired in the absence of the laws, minimum wages will decrease family income inequality. The latter effect seems to predominate, at least in recent American experience, and the minimum wage is a modest counterforce to rising inequality. But compared to European nations, in particular, American minimum wages are generally low, and until the federal minimum was raised by 1996 legislation, had been drifting downward (in inflation-adjusted terms) for nearly two decades. This erosion has probably contributed to overall wage inequality, especially among women.

During the most recent debate over raising the federal minimum, some opponents argued that the national floor under wages should be abolished, or greatly weakened, in favor of state-by-state decisions about whether and how aggressively to constrain low-end labor markets. The enemies of a national minimum based their arguments on both normative and empirical grounds. Since political values are embedded in minimum-wage policy (or its absence) and since political values differ from state to state, advocates of decentralized wage policy argue that each state should be able to tailor its policies to match its own particular alloy of egalitarianism and laissez-faire. And since states differ considerably in prevailing wage levels and industrial structure, state-specific minimums would avoid the risk of a uniform national minimum that is irrelevant in high-wage states and destructively high in low-wage states. Defenders of a national standard counter that states would find it exceedingly difficult to maintain minimum wages that have any appreciable effect on what low-paid workers actually collect. A state staking out a minimum wage higher than other states required—if low-wage employers have any choice at all over where they locate or expand—would risk losing investment and employment to less demanding states.

In 1995, then-senator Nancy Landon Kassebaum buttressed her proposal for state rather than national wage policy by charging that this "race-to-the-bottom" argument was at odds with the facts. Some states already had their own minimum wages exceeding the federal floor, Kassebaum pointed out. This shows that interstate competition poses no barrier if some particular state, guided by its own political lights, opts for a state-specific floor under wages.[1]

Yet this reassuring observation is less conclusive than it appears to be. Four of the nine states with minimum wages exceeding the federal mandate—Connecticut, New Jersey, Massachusetts, and Alaska—ranked among the five states with the highest prevailing *market* wage levels, inviting the inference that legislated wage floors have far less practical effect than they would in low-wage states. If the state-specific minimum in fact requires few workers to be paid more than they would collect without any interventions in the labor market, the laws are more symbolic than real, and are only trivial irritations to footloose firms. Three of the others—Washington, Delaware, and Hawaii—were among the top fifteen states, in terms of average pay levels, suggesting a similar muted effect. Only in Oregon (ranked twenty-third in average pay) and Vermont (ranked thirty-fifth) does there appear to be the potential for state-specific minimums to push very hard against the economic fundamentals, or for political culture to do much heavy lifting in the face of competitive pressures from other states.[2] In short, the claim that any state whose citizens believed in a floor under hourly pay could maintain a meaningful minimum wage in the absence of federal law, remains highly debatable.

Unemployment Insurance

If the downside of state-based minimum wage policy is still mostly hypothetical—the federal minimum remains alive and well, for the time being—on the issue of unemployment insurance it is all too real. New Deal-era federal legislation requires every state to maintain some system of income insurance for workers who lose their jobs.[3] But states control crucial details. In particular, they exercise discretion over which workers are eligible for benefits—what degree of previous attachment to the labor force workers must document, for example. The reason for suspecting that competitive dynamics will work against generous unemployment compensation is that the premiums are paid by employers.[4] Indeed, unemployment insurance (UI) premiums are one of the more significant business costs directly attributable to state policy decisions, and thus among the instruments of state strategy with the greatest competitive leverage. Corporate income taxes are frequently the focus of public debates over the burden on business. Yet while states and cities collected a total of around $28 billion in corporate income taxes in fiscal 1994—the most recent year for which complete data are available—the states collected $30 billion in UI premiums

The UI bill paid by a particular employer depends, to a limited degree, on its own history of workforce instability. Premiums are "experience rated"—adjusted up or down to reflect a firm's demonstrated propensity to dispatch its workers to the unemployment office—but variance in rates fails to fully reflect variance in risk, and the least stable employers pay only modestly more than the most stable employers. In greater part, the UI burden firms face depends on the total costs incurred by the state's UI system. And those costs, in turn, are greatly affected by state policy decisions.

It is standard practice, endorsed by federal rules, for states to require some kind of demonstrated attachment to the workforce as a condition for collecting unemployment benefits, to prevent casual or deliberately episodic workers from tapping the system unfairly. Similarly, for perfectly defensible reasons states have usually required some proof that a worker has become unemployed involuntarily (instead of simply quitting to collect benefits) and is able and willing to take a job if one becomes available. But these generic constraints on eligibility can take on a wide range of specific manifestations. If a state opts for relatively open eligibility standards, the vast majority of workers will find that they can actually collect benefits if they lose their jobs—and the premiums that employers must pay will be correspondingly burdensome. If a state opts for complex and restrictive eligibility standards, many unemployed workers will find themselves excluded from benefits—and the system's cost to employers will be correspondingly slight.

Whether internal state politics—reckoned without reference to interstate competition for business—will tilt toward generosity or austerity depends on cultural factors, on the balance of economic interests within a state, and on the deftness with which workers and managers play their political cards. But if workers greatly outnumber managers and owners, if most workers can imagine circumstances where they might be unemployed, and if workers perceive the cost of UI premiums to fall on employers, the normal product of politics alone would be a reasonably generous UI system.

But interstate competition for business can constrain, or even trump, internal politics. The more footloose firms become, and the more heavily do relative UI costs weigh in business location and expansion decisions, the greater the handicap imposed by open UI eligibility rules on a state's economic development. And the more states are invited to chart their own economic paths—and required by Washington's retreat to get by on their own resources—the more perilous it becomes to incur capital's displeasure. The stage is thus set for competitive reductions in unemployment benefits. Such a scenario risks increasing income inequality directly—since UI benefits, like other cash transfers, count as income—but also, and perhaps more importantly, by indirect means. As the odds of collecting unemployment benefits diminish, job loss looms as a financial catastrophe, rather than a manageable setback cushioned by insurance, and workers may logically become more timid about pressing for raises and promotions.

Just this scenario appears to be at work. A staff study for the federal Advisory Committee on Unemployment Compensation found that between 1978 and 1990—roughly coinciding with the broader shift toward the states—the fraction of unemployed Americans actually eligible for benefits under state rules has declined.[5] Some of the whittling away of UI eligibility reflects cost-shifting efforts by the states; if workers could be nudged away from the unemployment compensation system and onto food stamps, or some other arrangement where Washington pays the bills, the burden on employers could be lightened without inflicting much suffering on the workers themselves. But some of the shift also reflects pure competitive pressures, and as the menu of federal programs to which costs can be shifted shortens, the temptation to simple austerity is likely to intensify. The staff study estimates that between 1987 and 1993, efforts by states to match or undercut others states' UI costs shaved the average premium by 0.43 percent of payroll—no small reduction, since the typical baseline premium is in the range of 2.5 percent.[6] The dark side of this downward pressure on premiums, of course, is that fewer than one in every three jobless workers was actually collecting benefits in 1995.[7] It is instructive to note that the United States and Canada adopted similar systems of unemployment insurance at similar points in time. But the Canadian system was and remains centralized, and mostly immune to competition among the provinces. Today, Canadian unemployment insurance is considerably more inclusive than its American counterpart.[8]

Right-to-Work Laws

Labor organization has been in free-fall since the early 1980s. Even the Democratic Leadership Council—conventionally, if not quite accurately, considered the nemesis of organized labor within the Democratic Party—contends that shared prosperity will remain elusive without a revitalized union movement adapted to the economy's modern challenges.[9] Yet the prospects for such a renaissance remain in doubt, in part because of the fragmentation of policy over workplace organization.

Labor organization represents a classic example of what economists term a "collective action" problem. Consider any costly enterprise promising common benefits—deterring foreign aggression, or reducing the risk of global warming, or organizing employees to gain bargaining leverage in the workplace. Unless the costs can be made common as well, the prospect that some will "free ride" on the efforts of others shrinks the odds that the enterprise will occur. To defend our shores, for example, we require all to support the common effort through taxation. We are still struggling to find a way to define and enforce a fairly shared pattern of present sacrifice to reduce global warming in the future. Likewise, if all workers at a firm share in the benefits of collective bargaining, whether or not they take any initiative to organize, then only fools or martyrs will accept the risk and cost of unionizing a workplace. (A duly certified union must represent the interests of all workers in the "bargaining unit," whether members or not.) Fools and martyrs being rare as they are, allowing unions the right to exact support from all affected workers raises the probability of workplace organization.

The National Labor Relations Act of 1935 fortified organized labor in many ways, not least by strengthening unions' ability to require all employees at an organized workplace to either join the union or to support its services financially. Twelve years later, the Taft-Hartley Act weakened the NLRA—or, depending on one's perspective, adapted it to the special imperatives of American federalism—by allowing states to opt out of some key provisions. In particular, Taft-Hartley declared that state legislatures could pass laws banning "union shop" provisions in labor contracts, which require new employees to join (or at least contribute financially to) a union representing the firm's workers. In a linguistic triumph, these state-specific retreats from the NLRA are termed "right-to-work" laws. Tortuous scholarly explanations of the collective action problem have an uphill battle against the "right to work" in a culture as wary as ours is about any whiff of coercion.

One can construct a straightforward account of the incentives introduced by the state-specific policies on workplace organization, and craft a scenario for what ought to occur in a context of interstate competition for capital. The first step in the story is that unionization will wither in right-to-work states: Just as it would be hard to maintain an armed defense if neither taxation nor conscription were allowed, it will be hard to form a union if members and free riders share equally in the benefits. Next, as workers lose bargaining leverage, wage levels in right-to-work states will fall and profits will increase. Businesses that aren't rooted to any particular state will notice the greener pastures for profit-making in the right-to-work states and will flock to them, shunning states without such laws. These holdout states, in turn, will suffer depressed rates of investment and job growth. As the investment penalty for failure to adopt right-to-work laws is brought home to state politicians and voters, labor's leverage over internal political debates will weaken, and state after state will shift to the right-to-work camp. And finally, assuming unions are on balance an equalizing force, economic inequality will increase nationwide, with the early right-to-work states in the vanguard.

It turns out, however, that reality has not quite followed this script. The most obvious departure from expectations concerns timing. A surge of states passed right-to-work laws almost immediately after the Taft-Hartley Act cleared the way; by 1950, there were eleven right-to-work states. But in defiance of what the interstate competition scenario predicts, the surge soon slowed to a trickle. There are only twenty-one right-to-work states today, and only three states have adopted right-to-work laws since 1960. These include Wyoming (1963), Louisiana (1976), and Iowa (an original right-to-work state that enacted new legislation in 1986). Indiana adopted a right-to-work law in 1957, but repealed it eight years later.[10] Nor does the rest of the pattern neatly fit predictions. True, union membership is low in right-to-work states—under 13 percent in 1983, dropping to under 9 percent by 1995. And the right-to-work states have lower average annual earnings but a significantly faster growth rate for gross state product—both consistent with the logic outlined above. But union membership actually fell by a bit *less* in the right-to-work states than it did in the other states between 1983 and 1995. And the right-to-work states, as a group, display no more economic inequality—defined as the ratio of top-quintile to bottom-quintile family income—than do states *without* right-to work laws. (See Figure 7.1, pages 58–59).

What explains the mismatch between these patterns and the scenario, outlined above, of states defensively adopting right-to-work laws, driving down unionization and driving up inequality? One possibility is that the scenario is simply wrong. It could be that unionization *doesn't* tend to raise wages or reduce income inequality. Perhaps right-to-work laws *don't* discourage labor organization, so business has no reason to favor right-to-work states. Or maybe businesses' preference for laws handicapping unions is a feeble political force, because so few firms are really mobile, or because labor coalitions are a sufficiently heavy counterweight to the threat of lost investment. Another possibility, however, is that the scenario sketched out earlier forms only one part of a far more complex reality.

One complicating factor is the risk of confusing the effects of state-specific *laws* with other features of a state's economy, politics, or culture that affect growth, unionization, earnings, and inequality. Many analysts have argued that right-to-work laws have more symbolic than practical significance; in themselves they don't render a state inhospitable to organized labor, but merely affirm the preexisting strength of antiunion sentiments. By this view the mere passage of such laws is a minor matter; a state's basic orientation toward organized labor runs deeper and has its effects whether or not a pro- or antiunion stance is encoded into law.[11] If this is the case, there would be little reason for states to adopt right-to-work laws in the name of improving their attractiveness to business, and no reason to expect competitive pressures to produce a proliferation of formal state policies hostile to organized labor.

Steven E. Abraham and Paula B. Voos attempt to disentangle the *specific* impact of right-to-work laws from broader economic and cultural factors by examining the effects of *new* state laws discouraging unionization on the stock prices of firms located within a state. Other

FIGURE 7.1

RIGHT-TO-WORK STATES HAVE FASTER ECONOMIC GROWTH AND LOWER AVERAGE INCOME THAN OTHER STATES . . .

FIGURE 7.1A
AVERAGE ANNUAL INCREASE IN GROSS STATE PRODUCT, 1987–94, RIGHT-TO-WORK AND OTHER STATES

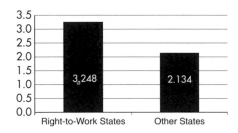

Source: Calculated from Census data at http://www.stat-usa.gov/BEN/ebb1/reg/gsp.bea; GSP data on quarterly basis; revised 1997.

FIGURE 7.1B
1994 AVERAGE ANNUAL EARNINGS, RIGHT-TO-WORK AND OTHER STATES

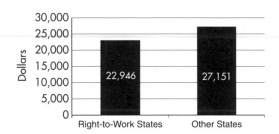

Source: Bureau of Labor Statistics data from http://www.census.gov:80/statb/ranks/pg19.txt.

FIGURE 7.1 CONTINUED

BUT RIGHT-TO-WORK STATES HAVE NO LARGER DROP IN UNION MEMBERSHIP FROM THE MID-1980s TO THE MID-1990s AND (AS A GROUP) NO HIGHER INCOME INEQUALITY

FIGURE 7.1c
DECLINES IN UNION MEMBERSHIP, 1983–95

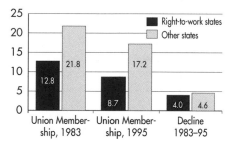

Source: Barry Hirsch and David Macpherson, *Union Membership and Earnings Data Book: Compilations from the Current Population Survey* (Washington, D.C.: Bureau of National Affairs, 1996), from U.S. Department of Commerce, Bureau of the Census, *Statistical Abstract of the United States 1997* (Washington, D.C.: U.S. Government Printing Office, 1997), Table 683.

FIGURE 7.1 D
RATIO OF TOP-QUINTILE TO BOTTOM-QUINTILE FAMILY INCOME, 1991–93

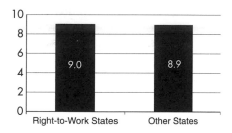

Source: Current Population Survey state-level data compiled by Jon Haveman of Purdue University and the Council of Economic Advisors and supplied to the author.

researchers have found that a union victory in a representation election lowers the value of the affected firm's stock by around 4 percent,[12] so it seems reasonable to expect that new state laws reducing the odds of such an event occurring would *increase* stock prices. Conversely, if right-to-work laws don't weaken labor, but merely reflect labor's underlying weakness, shareholders gain nothing extra from the passage of such laws and there should be no impact on stock values.

Only two states have enacted right-to-work laws since detailed daily stock-price data have been available—Louisiana in 1976 and Iowa in 1986. Shareholder returns for firms heavily affected by the two new right-to-work statutes increased, by something on the order of 2 to 3 percent, relative to movements in the stock market as a whole.[13] This is not at all what one would expect if the legislation merely symbolized a preexisting hostility toward organized labor within a state.

David Ellwood and Glenn Fine employ a very different approach to identify the independent impact of right-to-work laws. Instead of drawing inferences from stock prices, they look directly at the pace of workplace organization within each state. To isolate the effect of the legislation from other factors, they statistically control for separate economic, demographic, and political characteristics that might constrain or condition labor's clout. They also focus carefully on the *timing* of right-to-work legislation, reasoning that if background factors that somehow escape their statistical controls—rather than the laws themselves—are what affect workplace organization, then the passage of right-to-work laws should not cause a sharp departure from recent trends in union activity. Ellwood and Fine discover that new right-to-work laws *do* seem to stifle unionization in the decade after passage, especially in the first five years.[14] The effect on the *rate* of new union organization seems to level off over time, though Ellwood and Fine suggest that right-to-work laws have a durable effect on the *level* of worker unionization within a state. These two studies provide some reassurance that right-to-work laws can tilt the balance away from organized labor, but only deepen the puzzle of why unionization rates have dropped no faster in right-to-work states than in other states, and why so few states have adopted such laws in recent decades.

What about the fact that the right-to-work states display no worse inequality than states with more union-friendly laws? If right-to-work laws do, on balance, discourage unionization, and unionization does, on balance, reduce inequality, this isn't what we should see. More detailed assessment of the evidence is needed to resolve the issue, but one hint may be offered by looking separately at two subgroups of right-to-work states. Eight of the twenty-one are sparsely populated, heavily rural states in the Great Plains and mountain regions—the Dakotas, Iowa, Kansas, Idaho, Nebraska, Utah, and Wyoming. Major urban areas (whose slums and financial centers accentuate income inequality) are conspicuously rare in these eight states, which have an average ratio of top-quintile to bottom-quintile family income of a little under 7. The other right-to-work states have an average top-to-bottom ratio of 10.2, compared to the average for non-RTW states of just under 9. So while the answer awaits more systemic research, it seems likely that any impact of right-to-work laws on inequality is masked by the special economic and demographic characteristics of the Plains and mountain states.

What should we make of the whole tangled picture? Here is an attempt at accounting for the facts: The American labor movement's slow retreat from its postwar glory days turned into a headlong rout in the 1980s. Union membership plummeted from around 20 percent of the workforce in 1983 to around 14 percent in 1997.[15] One cause of this decline has been global integration, deregulation, and stepped-up structural change within the economy that has shrunk labor's stronghold in the manufacturing sector. Another cause has been federal policies under Bush and Reagan broadly antagonistic to organized labor. And another has been institutional torpor and strategic blunders on the part of the labor movement itself, as it concentrated (until recently) on slowing its losses in traditional industries and building a shaky new base in the public sector, instead of scrambling to organize the more dynamic parts of the private economy. Within this hurricane of antilabor forces, state right-to-work laws have been largely superfluous. The first round of right-to-work laws passed after the Taft-Hartley Act had already had its impact prior to the 1980s, and the collapse of worker power nationwide meant there was relatively little reason for business interests to push for the adoption of such laws in other states.

By this interpretation, the scenario of competitive pressures among the states to adopt right-to-work is not so much erroneous as irrelevant. States *can* take steps to handicap unions. Competitive imperatives *can* raise the odds they will do so. But with the labor movement so effectively crippled nationwide, businesses have little incentive to set the scenario in motion. One implication, should something like this explanation prove accurate, is that the prospect of state legislation is a latent check against the labor movement's resurgence. If organized labor manages to reclaim a measure of its vigor, and gains some success in shaping federal policy in its favor, a new round of state-level measures to accommodate mobile capital would erect a second line of defense against worker power.

8

EDUCATION FINANCE

What will determine the degree of economic inequality in the America of 2025? No honest person can answer that question with confidence. A quarter-century of political, economic, and technological change will surely overmatch our capacity to imagine the future. Some factors that no doubt will matter, such as trends in family structure, are hard to predict and even harder, perhaps, to alter through policy. Yet one factor appears all but certain to influence the degree of inequality a generation hence and is squarely connected to policy decisions—the level and distribution of investments in education and training over the next ten or fifteen years.

Indeed, "education and training" frequently figure in proposed solutions to a range of America's problems, not only (not even mainly) widening income inequality. As consensus crystallizes around the urgency of improving schools, universities, and community colleges, commentators jostle to put before the public their favorite road map for reaching that desirable destination. And given the attention fixed on the goal, we have decent odds of finding a path to improved education. Yet (as will be discussed shortly) there are some serious uncertainties about the fiscal resources to fuel the journey.

There is nothing new about the link between education and earning power. But the significance of skills, relative to other elements of the economic equation, has grown in pace with technical change and

the integration of the world economy. Competition from labor overseas, or from smart machines domestically, erodes the earning power
of unskilled workers. Fewer jobs require only a strong back or a large
capacity for boredom. New occupations generally call for advanced
skills, and even traditional occupations are being redefined in ways
that heighten the importance of human capital.

The paycheck penalty a changing economy imposes on the
unskilled has grown sharply in recent decades. Between 1973 and 1993,
families headed by high-school dropouts had a 30 percent fall in real
income (adjusted for family size). Families gained 17 percent over the
period, on average, if headed by someone with three or four years of
postsecondary education, and 31 percent if the family head had a college degree or further formal schooling.[1] For both men and women,
education dramatically affects earning power. (See Figures 8.1 and 8.2.)

FIGURE 8.1 MEAN INCOME OF MALES AGE TWENTY-FIVE AND OLDER, BY EDUCATIONAL ATTAINMENT, 1997

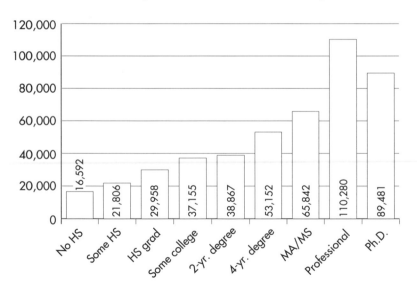

Source: U.S. Department of Commerce, Bureau of the Census Bureau, *Historical Data from the Current Population Survey*, Historical Income Tables (Persons), Table P-15: "Educational Attainment—People 25 Years Old and Over by Mean Income and Gender—1991 to 1997" (www.census.gov/hhes/income/histinc/p15, accessed January 1999).

**FIGURE 8.2 MEAN INCOME OF FEMALES AGE TWENTY-FIVE
AND OLDER, BY EDUCATIONAL ATTAINMENT, 1997**

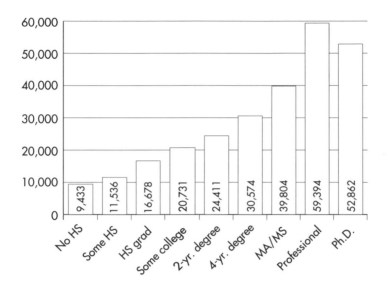

Source: U.S. Department of Commerce, Bureau of the Census Bureau, *Historical Data from
the Current Population Survey,* Historical Income Tables (Persons), Table P-15: "Educational
Attainment—People 25 Years Old and Over by Mean Income and Gender—1991 to 1997"
(www.census.gov/hhes/income/histinc/p15, accessed January 1999).

While the conventional hazards of prediction apply, I submit this
assessment of the choice before us: If most of the children born since,
say, 1990 get high-quality primary and secondary schooling followed
by more advanced training suited to their aptitudes and to the demands
of the labor market, then as these children grow into their prime earning years income gaps will tend to narrow. Universally good elementary
and secondary schools will equip students for appropriate postsecondary education. This, in turn, will raise the prevailing level of productivity, including the capacity of those who would otherwise (because
of limited innate talent, family disadvantages, or bad luck) produce
and earn less. An abundance of educated workers, meanwhile, will
whittle down the scarcity premium that has sent top workers' earnings soaring. Over the course of two or three decades—and in the
absence of unpredictable developments that would undercut the

benefits of human-capital investment—more and better education will narrow the income distribution, and narrow it at a relatively high level. Conversely, if American education falls short (so that luck, connections, and inborn abilities determine citizens' life prospects) or if some children and young adults get a much greater quantity and quality of education than others, then (unless there are improbably large counterforces in the other direction) income disparities will be wider in 2025 than they are today.

Investing in human capital across the whole population may be the only aggressive strategy for blunting the trend toward inequality that is consistent with American values. Simple redistributive transfers tend to grate against our notions of fairness. But public spending to build willing workers' earning power generally commands popular legitimacy, not least because of the value Americans traditionally place on the noneconomic benefits of an educated citizenry. As a bonus, adopting a skill-based strategy lets us dodge the intellectually vexing and politically incendiary issue of whether it is mostly global integration, or mostly technological change, that is producing such large disparities in productivity and earnings. The same prescription (broad-based human capital investment) follows from either diagnosis.

Whether we adopt that prescription, however, will depend heavily on state-level policy choices. During the 1994–95 school year, measured education spending in America came to about a half-trillion dollars. (A great deal of human-capital investment—including on-the-job training, parents' helping their children with homework, and the time students devote to learning, instead of playing or making money—inevitably goes unmeasured.) State budgets were the largest single funding source. (See Figure 8.3.)

Most directly relevant to the future trajectory of income inequality is spending at *public* institutions, which account for a little over 80 percent of the total. (See Figure 8.4.) The bulk of the schooling that goes on in America, particularly for children and young people from the lower-four income quintiles, occurs at public institutions. Some middle-class and less affluent children attend parochial primary and secondary schools, and quite a few attend private postsecondary institutions. But most rely on public schools, colleges, and universities. And for these institutions as a group, the states—which provide 44 cents out of every dollar—are considerably more important than local

FIGURE 8.3 FUNDING SOURCES FOR
ALL EDUCATIONAL INSTITUTIONS, 1994–95

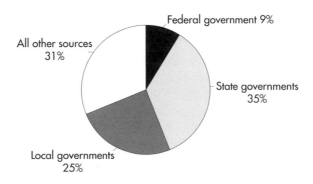

Sources: U.S. Department of Education, National Center for Education Statistics, Common Core of Data; Higher Education General Information Survey, "Financial Statistics of Institutions of Higher Education"; Integrated Postsecondary Education Data System (IPEDS) "Finance" survey, as published in U.S. Department of Education, *Digest of Education Statistics 1997,* Table 33, "Estimated total expenditures of educational institutions, by level, control of institution, and source of funds: 1979–80 to 1994–95" (nces.ed.gov/pubs/digest97/d97t033).

FIGURE 8.4 FUNDING SOURCES FOR PUBLIC
EDUCATIONAL INSTITUTIONS, 1994–95

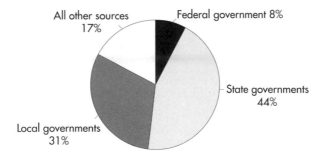

Sources: U.S. Department of Education, National Center for Education Statistics, Common Core of Data; Higher Education General Information Survey, "Financial Statistics of Institutions of Higher Education"; Integrated Postsecondary Education Data System (IPEDS) "Finance" survey, as published in U.S. Department of Education, *Digest of Education Statistics 1997,* Table 33, "Estimated total expenditures of educational institutions, by level, control of institution, and source of funds: 1979–80 to 1994–95" (nces.ed.gov/pubs/digest97/d97t033).

government, the federal government, or funding by parents, foundations, or other sources. State policy, moreover, greatly affects spending by local governments, the second largest source overall and a particularly important player in primary and secondary education.

So unless there are fundamental changes in the structure of American education, the level and distribution of investment in the next generation's productive skills will be determined to a great extent by the states. Like the value of human capital itself, the states' role in education finance is not new. What has changed are the stakes. As their autonomy grows and their other burdens multiply, will the separate states prove able and willing to fund education adequately in the decade to come?

Before going any further, I must acknowledge the objection (much in vogue in certain quarters) that this is a silly question. Many commentators, even some who profess great concern for American education, declare that money is simply not the issue. One variant of this argument starts with the claim that intelligence, aptitude for learning, and productive potential are predestined by one's genetic inheritance, or are so powerfully influenced by cultural and familial factors that good schools can't help much and bad schools can't hurt much. Another variant—less fatalistic, but a bit more cynical—concedes that good schools and colleges *could*, in principle, work improvements on the fresh clay of young minds. But absent scorched-earth restructuring, by this view, good schools and colleges are a pipe dream. Primary and secondary schools are layered with bureaucratic fat and infested with third-rate teachers entrenched by union rules and arrogantly contemptuous about quality, while colleges and universities are more concerned with esoteric research and aberrant cultural enthusiasms than with education. The solution lies not in more or better-targeted funding, but in revolutionary change.

There is something behind such sentiments. No interested observer of American education can dismiss the assertion that waste, irresponsibility, and indifference to excellence are dismayingly common, and nothing in this essay is inconsistent with the spirit of reform. Moreover, it is indeed quite difficult to prove that more resources equals better education. The quality of education is itself hard to define and measure. Do we go by students' standardized test scores? Or by how much additional education they pursue and how they fare in college? Or by their earning power five, ten, or twenty years out?

Or by some more comprehensive measure that goes beyond narrow economic benefits? The broader and longer-term the metric of educational outcomes, the harder becomes the measurement problem. And however we choose to define educational outcomes, factors other than funding—students' innate ability, the commitment to education of their families, their classmates, and their *classmates'* families; the quality of school governance—assuredly do affect results. The complexity of the link between money and outcomes explains the spirited debate among empiricists as to how and why money matters for education.[2]

The assertion that money doesn't matter much is, in part, simply one side of an honest intellectual disagreement. But it also serves as a shrewd rhetorical tactic on the part of those who see little benefit to themselves from public education spending, or who (whether out of sincere ardor for reform or a political or cultural animus against public schools and universities) seek to undermine American education in anything like its current form.

The tactic is reminiscent of one long employed by the Pentagon's political opponents in the budgetary struggle: First, runs the argument, you must prove that more military spending can really improve security. *Then* prove that every valid reform idea has been adopted and every bit of waste has been wrung from the system. *Then* we can talk about more resources for defense. Like the critics of education today, the military's critics have had excellent grounds for their complaints at virtually any point in our history. But had we accepted the challenge on their terms we would never have spent much on the armed forces. Any veteran of World War II, for example, can recount hair-raising tales of waste and inefficiency. But it doesn't follow that the enterprise wasn't worth it.

So I do not deny that human capital development depends on a great deal aside from money. Nor am I in the least unsympathetic to the case for reform in primary, secondary, and postsecondary education. But I am persuaded that the level of resources available to schools and colleges does affect the odds for good educational outcomes. Anyone convinced to the contrary, of course, will find the rest of this essay to be profoundly uninteresting.

Even those willing to grant that money matters for education, and that education matters for future inequality, might sensibly object that there is little to worry about. Public spending per pupil in the United States is at or near the top of the range among OECD countries, after all, and was 15 percent higher (in real terms) during the 1996–97 school year than it had been ten years previously. Total state and local education spending has been stable or rising as a share of both gross domestic product or personal income. And in recent years (as of this writing) there has been a veritable budgetary bonanza for education in the state capitals. In the mid-1990s state budgets for both K–12 and postsecondary spending generally grew faster than spending overall, and much faster than inflation. On average, states increased allocations for primary and secondary education by 6.2 percent and for higher education by 5.8 percent between fiscal 1997 and 1998.[3] In the election year of 1998 the flood of new money quickened. As fiscal 1999 budgets took shape, estimates of the average increase in education funding ranged up to 7 percent.[4]

Local governments' share of primary and secondary school budgets had fallen in the 1980s in response to tax-limitation movements, court orders to equalize spending, and a consequent increase in state aid. The local share rebounded with state cutbacks in the early 1990s. But in the mid-1990s the states were once again bearing a growing share of the burden, partly due to state budget surpluses, and partly due to a new round of court orders. (Over the past two decades there have been eighteen state supreme court decisions declaring locally based school finance systems unconstitutional.)[5] Bulging state coffers combined with top officials' political ambitions inspired especially large increases in per-pupil education budget proposals in New York, Michigan, and several other states, both boosting resources overall and shrinking disparities between richer and poorer districts.[6] In such a setting one risks appearing immune to the evidence, and churlish to boot, by suggesting that the states could worsen long-term income inequality by dropping the ball on education.

Yet there are four basic causes for concern on this score: The surge in expected enrollment, the dwindling of funding from local and federal governments, the vulnerability of the budget surpluses that are fueling recent state spending growth, and the latent political fragility of states' commitment to broad-based education investment.

RISING DEMAND

Until very recently, the era of growing income inequality has coincided with stable or falling burdens on American schools. The 1980s were the eye of the demographic hurricane. The baby-boom generation had mostly completed its own education, but the children of this massive cohort—the baby boom echo—had not yet flooded the schools. Enrollments in primary and secondary schools were generally around 45 million through most of the decade—lower than at any time since the early 1960s, and down from a peak of over 51 million in the early 1970s. This lull is over. Student headcounts began trending upward again in the early 1990s. As immigrants join the baby boomers' offspring, the burdens on K–12 classrooms are expected to exceed the old record by decade's end and approach 55 million by 2006. (See Figure 8.5, p. 72.) The strain on postsecondary education is determined both by demographics and by the long rise in enrollment rates. While the number of students in college, graduate and professional schools, and community colleges has been rising fairly steadily since the 1960s, here, too, a quickening trend is under way. The number of postsecondary students is expected to rise by 1.5 million between 1998 and 2006.[7]

These are only projections, of course. For primary and secondary enrollments the predictions are not particularly perilous; the *quantity* of K–12 education is largely determined by demographics (though its *quality* responds to other factors.) Postsecondary enrollment is more uncertain, however. It will be affected by the perceived payoff to higher education, and by its cost. Over roughly the past two decades, rising tuition at state universities and community colleges, along with generally declining financial aid, has coincided with a widening gap in postsecondary enrollment rates between more- and less-affluent young people. There is evidence that rising out-of-pocket costs at community colleges, in particular, are already squeezing out some potential students from lower-income families.[8]

For American education overall, as student demand hits a sustained plateau during the first decade of the next century, there are only three possible responses: Efficiency will improve. Or spending will increase. Or quality and access will erode. It is hard to imagine anything with greater influence over income inequality in the next generation than the balance we strike, over the next decade or so, among these three responses.

FIGURE 8.5 TOTAL ENROLLMENT, 1980–96 (ACTUAL)
AND 1997–2006 (PROJECTED)

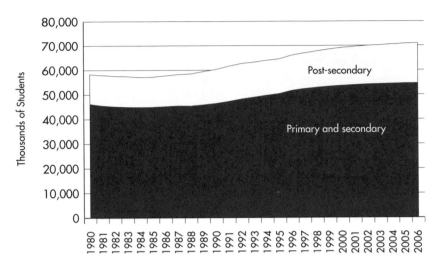

Sources: U.S. Department of Education, National Center for Education Statistics, *Statistics of State School Systems; Statistics of Public Elementary and Secondary School Systems; Statistics of Nonpublic Elementary and Secondary Schools; Projections of Education Statistics to 2007; Common Core of Data; Higher Education General Information Survey* (HEGIS), "Fall Enrollment in Institutions of Higher Education" surveys; and Integrated Postsecondary Education Data System (IPEDS), "Fall Enrollment" surveys, as published in U. S. Department of Education, *Digest of Educational Statistics 1997*, Table 3, "Enrollment in educational institutions, by level and by control of institution" (nces.ed.gov/pubs/digest97/d97t003).

CONSTRAINTS ON OTHER SOURCES
OF EDUCATION FINANCE

In principle, local governments, the federal government, or private fees and contributions could compensate for any shortfall in state spending. When states last encountered budget problems in the late 1980s and early 1990s the mix of education funding—which had been moving toward the states since 1970—tilted back toward local governments, and a surge in federal aid propped up overall spending.[9] But there are reasons to doubt that this rescue will be repeated next time. The proliferation of statutory or constitutional limitations on local taxes, combined with court orders limiting district-specific education spending, combined with local political trends (such as opposition by childless voters or retirees on fixed incomes) constraining taxes to pay for schools, renders unlikely the notion of sustained increases in local spending on primary and secondary education.[10] And local governments have never been prominent sources of funds for postsecondary institutions, the category for which rising demand, vulnerability to resource shortfalls, and the link to disparities of earning power are arguably greatest.

Meanwhile, statutory federal spending limits, and the evolution away from "categorical" grants that rise with need and toward fixed "block grants," mean that total intergovernmental transfers from Washington are slated for stagnation, in real terms, into the next century. Medicaid will claim a growing share of this limited pool, and there is little prospect under current law that rising federal grants would counter a reduction in state education resources. Real federal spending on education itself is actually predicted to *decline** in the early years of the century.[11]

Inadequate public budgets for education *could* inspire a historically unprecedented increase in *private* spending, most likely in the context of a major tilt toward private schools. Private institutions, which are generally more reliant on fees and private grants than are public institutions, already account for over one-fifth of the postsecondary enrollment in the United States (though the likelihood of attending a private college or university tends to rise or fall with family income). There are increasingly insistent proposals for a massive shift to private K–12 education—fueled by vouchers and tax credits—as a superior alternative to improving the public schools.

But setting aside for now the high-voltage politics surrounding this issue, consider the feasibility of effecting such a transformation in time to affect the next generation's endowment of human capital. The number of students in private elementary and secondary schools has ranged between 5.2 and 5.7 million for the past two decades or so. Most private K–12 institutions are religious schools, with limited capacity or inclination to ramp up their operations in response to growing demand. There *is* an embryonic for-profit education industry, but its record is mixed, its potential is untested, and its current scale of operation is minuscule. Suppose, for the moment, that the most extravagant claims of private education's superiority were somehow proven true tomorrow; political opposition to headlong school privatization miraculously evaporated; and we resolved to have one-half of

* As this goes to press, the Clinton administration has proposed significant increases in federal education spending, though Congress has not yet concurred.

American children in private schools by 2005. The capacity of private elementary and secondary schools, which grew by around 500,000 between 1980 and 1997, would have to expand by more than 15 *million* over the next six years.[12] While this is not beyond the bounds of possibility, perhaps, it does not seem very likely to occur, even in the most implausibly favorable political environment. Nor, of course, is it at all clear that the consequences for future income inequality would be benign. It is all but certain that the human-capital investment for the next generation will take place primarily in public elementary and secondary schools, and in a mix of public and private postsecondary institutions, that is not strikingly different from what we see today.

THE PROSPECT OF FISCAL PRESSURE

As this is written, the fiscal giddiness induced by the long, powerful expansion of the 1990s is combining with election-year politics to generate both state tax cuts and large increases in state education spending. If our current prosperity turns out to be permanent, there may be little cause for concern about resources for the schools. But on the chance that the boom does *not* go on forever, it is worth considering the likely robustness of state education spending in the face of fiscal pressure.

On the plus side, the shift away from individual and corporate income taxes and toward consumption taxes (a shift noted and lamented earlier in this essay) *does* render state treasuries a bit less vulnerable to recession; sales tax revenues fall less drastically than income tax revenues when the economy slows. Yet most states still rely to a great degree on income taxes, which vary dramatically with the economic cycles, and most other categories of state revenue also slow or shrink somewhat in a downturn. The last economic slump in the early 1990s produced excruciating budget pressures and wrenching cutbacks in the states, and the next recession will likely do much the same. This effect will be exacerbated by the shift of policy burdens, notably welfare, from Washington to the states; by the constriction of federal grants in general and their evolution from categorical grants that vary with requirements into fixed block grants;[13] and by the latest cycle of competitive tax cutting at the state level.

If and when the states again encounter fiscal difficulties, it would not be easy for education to escape unscathed. Education is by far the largest component of state budgets, claiming about one-third of total general spending in 1996 and dwarfing every other category except "public welfare"—mostly Medicaid—which accounted for about one-quarter. Most of the other categories of state spending are either small (like corrections, at 4 percent) or difficult to reduce very much in response to bad times (like insurance trust payments, at 11 percent) or both (like interest, at 3 percent).[14] Education spending, conversely, can be adjusted as budgetary conditions require. Aid to local primary and secondary education can be scaled back, budgets for state universities and community colleges can be trimmed, or tuition can be increased and financial aid tightened. With few exceptions, the recent boosts in state education spending have been extraordinary increases rather than permanent shifts in funding formulae, and many have been explicitly labeled "one-time" bonuses in local school aid or postsecondary funds.

As Figure 8.6 shows, the pattern of state and local spending on education, across the cycles of boom and bust, suggests that decisions about resources for the schools have been at least as heav-

FIGURE 8.6 REAL CHANGES IN STATE AND LOCAL SPENDING (TOTAL AND EDUCATION ONLY) AND STUDENT ENROLLMENT, 1964–92

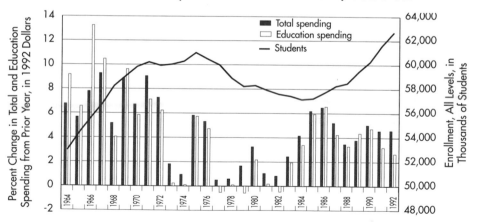

Sources: Calculated from *Digest of Education Statistics 1996,* Table 3, "Enrollment in Educational Institutions, by Level and by Control of Institution: 1869–70 to Fall 2006" (nces.ed.gov/pubs/d96/D96T003) and Table 36, "Gross Domestic Product, State and Local Expenditures, Personal Income, Disposable Personal Income, Median Family Income, and Population: 1929 to 1995" (nces.ed.gov/pubs/d96/D96T036).

ily affected by fiscal conditions as by educational imperatives. During the lean years of 1973 and 1974 real education spending dropped, even as enrollments drove to then-record levels. In the flush years of the mid-1980s, education spending rose (in pace with state and local spending overall) in spite of the fact that the number of students was relatively stable. And in the last round of budget pressure in the early 1990s, education spending slackened, despite surging enrollment. Figure 8.7 gives a tighter focus on state spending for postsecondary education alone, for a shorter time period. It demonstrates even more dramatically the disconnect between growing demand and resources in the budget crunch of the early 1990s, with the consequences noted earlier—rising tuition, shrinking aid, and a widening gap between more- and less-affluent students in the odds of enrolling in postsecondary education.[15]

For the moment, the supply of education resources and the demand for education capacity are rising in tandem. But unless the economy stays strong for a decade to come, the next state fiscal crisis

FIGURE 8.7 ANNUAL CHANGES IN STATE POSTSECONDARY SPENDING (IN CURRENT DOLLARS) AND POSTSECONDARY ENROLLMENT, 1976–93

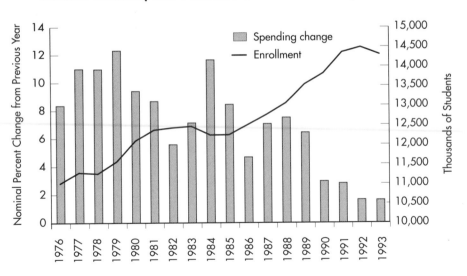

Sources: Calculated from *Digest of Education Statistics 1996,* Table 3, "Enrollment in Educational Institutions, by Level and by Control of Institution: 1869–70 to Fall 2006" (nces.ed. gov/pubs/d96/ D96T003) and Table 324, "Revenue of Institutions of Higher Education, by Source of Funds: 1919–20 to 1993–94" (nces.ed.gov/ pubs/d96/D96T324).

will coincide with historic highs in enrollment. Schools and colleges will have to compete with every other claim on shrinking state funds, including the imperative to match other states in tax restraint. The record is not reassuring about the likely consequences.

FRAGILE COMMITMENTS TO BROAD-BASED EDUCATION

Any review of state-of-the-state addresses will document that governors are fully aware both of education's political popularity and of the links between skills, productivity, and earning power. Moreover, the most pragmatic sort of economic development considerations would seem to ensure state-level enthusiasm for human-capital investment. Corporate CEOs attending the 1996 Governors' Education Summit committed themselves to "considering the quality of a state's academic standards . . . as a high-priority factor in determining business location decisions."[16] Empirical research has shown that productivity levels differ substantially from state to state, and that the skill level of a state's workforce is a significant determinant of its productivity.[17]

So why should we not expect prudent states to sow the seeds of future prosperity by investing heavily, through boom and bust alike, in education and training? Optimists can argue from economic, political, and historical grounds that states will shoulder their responsibilities for education and job training. But there are a number of depressingly logical reasons for state officials to skimp on schools and colleges, especially during a budget crunch. The most obvious is that education is usually a long-term investment. If a governor raises taxes to build schools or hire teachers or subsidize community college tuition, at the risk of repelling capital and angering voters, most of the benefit (higher productivity, incomes, and revenue) will fall in future administrations. Even when officials are utterly convinced of the merits of education and training, they may be reluctant to fund education at the expense of either short-term tax relief or competing spending with a more immediate payoff. (The proliferation of term-limit laws, already enacted in twenty-one states, may further foreshorten state officials' time horizons.)[18]

Timing aside, moreover, people aren't fixed assets. The case for a degree of *public* spending on education and training—instead of simply leaving skill building to the market—depends in part on the mobility of human capital, which weakens businesses' willingness to invest in worker skills. But mobility also dilutes the incentives of *states* to spend on education. Workers educated at the expense of one state can move away and apply their productive skills elsewhere. Roughly 3 percent of Americans relocate from one state to another each year. The more educated the individual, significantly, the more likely he or she is to leave the state. Consider Census Bureau mobility data for people twenty-five or older (to avoid the bias from newly minted college graduates heading off for their first jobs) covering the period from 1981 to 1994. Only 1.6 percent of high-school dropouts moved interstate each year compared to 2.2 percent of high-school graduates; 2.9 percent of workers with some postsecondary education; and 3.9 percent of college graduates.[19] In other words, if a state commits public resources to raise the odds that a worker completes a college degree instead of dropping out of high school, part of the reward is doubling the probability of losing that worker to another state. Ballot-box pressures will tend to counter this narrow economic calculus, to be sure. And both interstate mobility and the differential between more- and less-educated workers in the propensity to move, have been declining in recent years.[20] But the mobility of human capital clouds confident predictions that development-minded states will emphasize education.

Indeed, education austerity is sometimes linked directly to economic development campaigns. This seems puzzling, at first blush. Most businesses *are* in favor of better education, not least because most business people care about their communities. But businesses tend to be *directly* interested in a narrow segment of the education system, affecting their employees' children and their own specific human-capital needs. And prudent firms, no matter what their stakes in good schools, will always prefer that they themselves, and their key employees, pay as small a share as possible of the costs. The Albuquerque suburb of Rio Rancho, for example, lured the world's largest chip-making operation with a $114 million incentive package tailored to meet the list of priorities Intel had circulated to officials in several states. The package included publicly funded training, subsidies for relocation costs, reductions in corporate income taxes, and a thirty-year exemption from property taxes—the source of school funding. Despite a 64 percent increase in *individual* property taxes, the school district proved unable to fund school construction to meet swelling enrollments. As production got under way at the new Intel plant, most primary and middle-school students sat in trailers or in classrooms filled to double capacity, and plans to build the first high school for the 44,000-resident town were derailed by shortfalls in property tax revenue. (When a front-page *Wall Street Journal* article linked the Intel incentive package with Rio Rancho's foundering school system, Intel agreed to provide special support for local education.)[21] However compelling the logical link between education and development, it is no guarantee of adequate funding.

Education and training, moreover, have a distributional element that becomes more important as economic inequality deepens. In an earlier era of human-capital development, according to Claudia Goldin and Lawrence Katz, publicly funded education "enabled those from less fortunate circumstances to enter the higher-paying occupations of the early twentieth century."[22] The political climate prevailing in the late-nineteenth and early twentieth centuries proved conducive to aggressive state spending on education—even though some of the benefits fell out of state, and even though the wealthy often carried a disproportionate burden of paying for the schools that mattered most to their less fortunate fellow citizens. In the aftermath of World War II, gratitude toward veterans and the fear of a labor surplus combined to produce the G.I. Bill, which triggered a surge in postsecondary education that helped to drive down inequality in the postwar decades. The politics of broad-based human-capital development can play out differently, as Thomas Jefferson learned to his sorrow. Education was close to Jefferson's heart; he directed that his epitaph record his founding of the University of Virginia, rather than his presidency of the United States. But one of Jefferson's earlier forays into education reform foundered on the politics of inequality. Jefferson had proposed for Virginia a public education system modeled on common-school innovations in New England. But the initiative failed, two historians record, in large part because "the Virginia elite, on whom the bulk of the taxation would fall, had no intention of paying for the education of their poorer neighbors' children."[23]

The political tension inherent in education spending disproportionately funded by the well off and mobile, and disproportionately urgent for the less fortunate, could lead states to scale back their overall commitment to human-capital development. Still more likely is a selective retreat, de-emphasizing the equalizing mission of education and training. The starkest pressures, in any case, remain to be faced, including the full effects of the ongoing campaign of tax cuts and the fiscal damage that an economic downturn or two will inflict on state budgets.

9

CONCLUSION

This generation of Americans confronts the challenge of shoring up our middle-class culture in a world grown rather inhospitable to that heritage. Our successors will judge us by whether we succeed or fail at this task—unless our failure is so complete that the future finds small meaning in the middle-class values we cherish today. It is by no means assured (however we structure our public sector) that America's magnificent achievement of broadly shared prosperity will survive. But government's shift toward the states will worsen the odds. Amid the confluence of demographic, technological, and economic forces that are driving up income inequality, our current enthusiasm for fragmented government is exquisitely ill-timed.

If the story laid out here is anywhere near correct, a number of potential policy implications follow. Rather than continuing the trend toward fiscal decentralization, we should move toward the model prevailing in most other federations (where a large fraction of public revenue is raised centrally but spent locally) to help reverse the regressive slide in the overall structure of taxation. As evidence accumulates on the grand experiment in state-based antipoverty policy, we should harvest every lesson and remain open to the conclusion that only nation-based policy can avoid a built-in bias toward harshness. To adapt America's labor policy to modern imperatives, we should take steps to reduce states' incentives for competitive reductions in

unemployment insurance and other worker benefits, and brace for
the emergence of new state right-to-work laws if and when the labor
movement again finds its footing.

Perhaps the most radical potential prescription is to reconsider
America's custom of decentralized financing for education and training. Debates over education finance have conventionally concerned
the proper balance between local property taxes and state taxes
(which are increasingly regressive, relative to federal revenues). But
nothing in our Constitution, and nothing in the logic of human-
capital investment, so narrowly constricts the options. Other choices
are open to us.

Public education funding makes no sense unless we assert a common interest in education. But our present financing arrangements
imply that this common interest stops abruptly at the city limits or
the state border. If we were designing afresh America's system of education finance, is it conceivable that we would rely so heavily upon
state and local revenues? Preparing Americans for responsible citi-
zenship and for rewarding roles in a changing economy—if we accept
this as a public mission at all—is in large measure a national mission,
warranting a larger role for national financing than tradition dictates.
Pooling the burden of educating the next generation through greater
federal funding, moreover, is consistent with almost any reform scenario, from public school choice to charter schools to vouchers. Let the
debate continue on how to improve the effectiveness and accountability of our schools, colleges, and universities. But meanwhile, we
should engage in a parallel debate on whether the national share of
public education spending should exceed the prevailing level of about
one dollar in eight.[1]

One possibility already under discussion is to dedicate part of
the projected federal budget surplus to support local school con-
struction or operations, or to improve access to colleges and universities. But there are other options to consider as well. An intriguing (if
admittedly provocative) possibility would be to supplement state and
local taxes on physical property with a national tax on financial property, the proceeds of which would be devoted (via vouchers, intergovernmental transfers, scholarships, or other means) to education.
Over the past ten years the value of noncorporate real estate—the
core tax base for local education funding—has increased by just over
50 percent, from about $6.2 trillion to about $9.5 trillion. Over the

same period the value of noncorporate *financial* property has grown two and a half times faster, from a little under $12 trillion to a little over $27 trillion.[2] Unlike real estate—especially residential property, which accounts for the bulk of middle-class wealth—holdings of financial property are heavily concentrated among the most fortunate families.[3] Also unlike real estate, financial property itself is almost entirely free of tax burdens in the United States (although its returns are generally, but not always, subject to taxation). The main exception is our notoriously unfair estate tax, which clamors for a more rational replacement.[4]

Like any tax, a financial property tax to supplement current sources of education funding would involve sacrifices and inefficiencies. Such a tax would be feasible only at the national level; a single city or a single state would find it virtually impossible to impose taxes on financial wealth. Even if levied nationally, anything but a tiny tax would risk driving capital to offshore shelters, or inspiring wasteful evasion maneuvers. But a tiny tax might do the trick. Financial holdings are large enough and concentrated enough to permit raising substantial revenues while exempting most families altogether, and while imposing maximum levies far below the level of 1, 2, or 3 percent that families commonly pay on the value of their homes.[5] Calculations by Edward Wolff, for example, suggest that a wealth tax exempting net worth below $250,000 and levied at a graduated rate topping out at 0.3 percent—an order of magnitude lower than typical residential property taxes—would raise about $50 billion a year.[6] This is around one-quarter as much as the annual revenue from local property taxes, or (for another base of comparison) about equal to the aggregate sum of state lottery proceeds devoted to education from 1964 through 1995.[7] Fifty billion dollars from earmarked financial property taxes would roughly double federal education spending. Such resources, adroitly targeted, could make a difference. A substantial and sustained increase in federal funding for education may be our best hope for curbing the risk that human-capital investment will fall short over the next ten years—a decade in which surging enrollment will likely coincide with both growing returns to skills and rising economic inequality.

While this would be a novel departure for American public finance, it is by no means obvious that a federal tax on financial property is a less fair or less efficient source of funds for education than a local tax on housing, a state tax on gasoline, or government profits from games of chance. Those who find this embryonic notion worth exploring further must establish that there is a practical and fair way to collect such a tax, and that the proceeds would in fact improve education and training (instead of being wasted, or substituted for other resources). These are not trivial tasks. But those inclined to summarily dismiss the idea carry equally heavy obligations. They must suggest a better idea than a national financial property tax for increasing human capital investment. Or a better idea than education and training for restoring shared prosperity. Or they must argue that current trends can continue unchecked without threatening anything essential about America.

It is conceivable, of course, that the growth of family income inequality will reverse itself, for reasons that nobody can predict and that have nothing to do with public policy. Or it may be that no economic downturn will ever again imperil state finances, so that the temptation to shortchange education or other public bulwarks against rising inequality will never materialize. Or the citizens of the separate states may prove determined to enact fifty sets of policies aimed at shared prosperity, even in the face of competitive pressures. But I hesitate to bet the future on it. And that, of course, is precisely what we are doing.

NOTES

2

1. Unless otherwise noted, the CPS data come from the Census Bureau's on-line version of *Historical Data from the Current Population Survey*, http://census.gov/hhes/income/histinc, which was revised in September 1997 and accessed between November 1997 and January 1999. The Labor Department's Bureau of Labor Statistics manages the CPS, but the Census Bureau does the legwork.

2. Inequality of *consumption* has also increased, with most of the growth in consumption inequality occurring in the 1980s. See David Johnson and Stephanie Shipp, "Trends in Inequality Using Consumer Expenditures: 1960 to 1993," *Proceedings of the Section on Survey Research Methods* (Alexandria, Va.: American Statistical Association, 1995).

3. All the figures in this paragraph and the next several are from *Historical Data from the Current Population Survey*, Table F-2, "Share of Aggregate Income Received by Each Fifth and Top 5 Percent of Families (All Races): 1947 to 1996." The discontinuous jump in 1993 in top-quintile and top-twentieth share of aggregate family income likely had something to do with procedural changes to the Current Population Survey put in place in 1994, including lifting the upper limits of income respondents could report, though nobody can argue that growing inequality is simply an artifact of the survey methods.

4. In fact, during the 1980s work hours for men age twenty-five to sixty-five actually increased by only one-tenth as much—3.2 percent versus 31 percent—among the best paid as they did among the worst paid, despite the fact that tax rates dropped for the former and rose for the latter. See Joel Slemrod and Jon Bakija, *Taxing Ourselves* (Cambridge and London: MIT Press, 1997), Table 4.2, p. 107.

5. Shares of personal income calculated from Council of Economic Advisors, *Economic Report of the President, 1997* (Washington: U.S. Government Printing Office, 1997), Table B-27.

6. Peter Gottschalk, "Inequality, Income Growth, and Mobility: The Basic Facts," *Journal of Economic Perspectives* 11, no. 2 (Spring 1997).

7. Ibid., Table 1, p. 37.

8. Ibid., p. 37, esp. notes 18 and 19.

9. Ibid., p. 38. See also Daniel P. McMurrer and Isabel V. Sawhill, *Getting Ahead: Economic and Social Mobility in America* (Washington, D.C.: Urban Institute Press, 1998), p. 34.

10. U.S. Department of Commerce, Bureau of the Census, *Detailed Historical Tables from the Current Population Survey (CPS) 1947–1996,* Experimental Measures, Table RDI-5, "Index of Income Concentration (Gini Index), by Definition of Income: 1979 to 1996" (www.census.gov/hhes/income/histinc/rdi05). The 1996 Gini coefficient for the standard measure of income was .447 in 1996; for the most comprehensive alternative definition of income (which includes imputed rent for owner-occupied housing as well as a long list of taxes and transfers) it was .392. In 1980, the Gini coefficient for conventionally defined income had been .401, and for the comprehensive definition it was .347. In other words, the Gini coefficient for conventional income increased by 11.5 percent over the period, and for the comprehensive measure of income, it increased by 13 percent.

11. These figures, based on 1996 dollars, are from *Detailed Historical Tables from the Current Population Survey (CPS) 1947–1996,* Table F-3, "Mean Income Received by Each Fifth and Top 5 Percent of Families (All Races): 1966 to 1996."

12. Council of Economic Advisors, *Economic Report of the President 1997* (Washington, D.C.: U.S. Government Printing Office, 1997), Table B-38.

13. Chinhui Juhn, "Relative Wage Trends, Women's Work, and Family Income," American Enterprise Institute Working Paper (1996), esp. Figures 6 and 7, pp. 12–13.

14. Peter Gottschalk and Timothy M. Smeeding, "Cross National Comparisons of Earnings and Income Inequality," *Journal of Economic Literature* 35, no. 2 (June 1997): 643–44, esp. Figure 1.

15. Calculated from *Economic Report of the President, 1997,* Tables B-1 and B-101.

16. Figures from "Foreign-Born and Total Population," Immigration and Naturalization Service website (http://www. ins.usdoj. gov/stats/308). It is worth noting that while the 1990 figure was a post-1950 high, it was considerably lower than that of any prior twentieth-century census.

17. If new immigrants tend to cluster at the low-income end of the scale, moreover, an increase in immigration will raise inequality even if the earnings of native workers aren't affected.

18. Richard B. Freeman, *When Earnings Diverge: Causes, Consequences, and Cures for the New Inequality in the U.S.* (Washington, D.C.: National Policy Association, 1997), p. 40.

19. George J. Borjas, "The Internationalization of the U.S. Labor Market and the Wage Structure," Federal Reserve Bank of New York, *Economic Policy Review*, January 1995, pp. 5–6, drawing on research from George Borjas, Richard B. Freeman, and Lawrence F. Katz, "On the Labor Market Impacts of Immigration and Trade," in Borjas and Freeman, eds., *Immigration and the Work Force* (Chicago: University of Chicago Press, 1992), and Borjas and Valerie A. Ramey, "Foreign Competition, Market Power, and Wage Inequality: Theory and Evidence," National Bureau of Economic Research Working Paper no. 4556 (1993).

20. Niels Thygesen, Yutaka Kosai, and Robert Z. Lawrence, *Globalization and Trilateral Labor Markets: Evidence and Implications* (New York, Paris, and Tokyo: Trilateral Commission, 1996). See also Gary Burtless, Robert Z. Lawrence, Robert E. Litan, and Robert J. Shapiro, *Globaphobia: Confronting Fears about Open Trade* (Washington, D.C.: Brookings Institution, Progressive Policy Institute, and Twentieth Century Fund, 1998).

21. Survey results sent to author by Alan Krueger.

22. Andrew B. Bernard and J. Bradford Jensen have found that the loss of manufacturing jobs was one of the main explanations of growing intrastate wage inequality during the 1980s. "Understanding Increasing *and* Decreasing Wage Inequality," paper prepared for National Bureau of Economic Research Conference on the Impact of International Trade on Wages, photocopy, January 1998.

23. The figures on personal income by educational attainment are from *Historical Data from the Current Population Survey,* Tables P-13 and P-14. The definition of educational attainment for post-1990 data differs from the earlier series, though the "postgraduate" figure for 1996 cited here is a weighted average of median income for men with doctoral, professional, and masters' degrees, making it reasonably comparable to the 1990 counterpart category.

24. Gottschalk, "Inequality, Income Growth, and Mobility," Figure 5, p. 31, traces the late-1970s dip in the education premium and its almost steady climb since the early 1980s.

25. *Historical Data from the Current Population Survey,* Tables P-13 and P-14.

26. For commentary and analysis on this issue, see George E. Johnson, "Changes in Earnings Inequality: The Role of Demand Shifts," *Journal of Economic Perspectives* 11, no. 2 (Spring 1997), esp. p. 51; Gottschalk, "Inequality, Income Growth, and Mobility," esp. Figure 5, p. 31; and

Thomas Kane, "Beyond Tax Relief: Long-Term Challenges in Financing Higher Education," *National Tax Journal* 50, no. 2 (1997): 336. The survey of economists by Ashenfelter and Krueger mentioned found an average of 44 percent of rising wage inequality attributed to new technologies.

27. Nicole M. Fortin and Thomas Lemieux, "Institutional Changes and Rising Wage Inequality: Is There a Linkage?" *Journal of Economic Perspectives* 11, no. 2 (Spring 1997): 94.

28. U.S. Department of Commerce, *Statistical Abstract of the United States, 1997* (Washington, D.C.: U.S. Government Printing Office, 1998), Table 688.

29. For a thorough exploration of this issue see David Card, "The Effect of Unions on the Structure of Wages: A Longitudinal Analysis," *Econometrica* 64, no. 4 (July 1996).

30. The economists surveyed by Ashenfelter and Krueger attribute an average of 9 percent of the growth in wage dispersion to falling unionization. Fortin and Lemieux (pp. 89–90, esp. Table 2) see lower organization rates as responsible for 21 percent of the increase in male wage dispersion between 1979 and 1988, though the effect for women is different, since many of the unionized women are relatively high-skilled public sector workers who would be well-paid in any event. Richard Freeman also finds that declining unionization accounts for about a fifth of the growing wage gap ("Labor Market Institutions and Earnings Inequality," *New England Economic Review* [May/June 1996]: 164) and *When Earnings Diverge: Causes, Consequences, and Cures for the New Inequality in the U.S.* (Washington, D.C.: National Policy Association, 1997), p. 40.

31. Gottschalk and Smeeding, "Cross National Comparisons of Earnings and Income Inequality," and Thomas J. Volgy, John E. Scharz, and Lawrence E. Imwalle, "In Search of Economic Well-Being: Worker Power and the Effects of Productivity, Inflation, Unemployment, and Global Trade on Wages in Ten Wealthy Countries," *American Journal of Political Science* 40, no. 4 (November 1996).

32. For a discussion of this theme, see Robert H. Frank and Philip J. Cook, *The Winner-Take-All Society* (New York: Free Press, 1995); also see Freeman, "Labor Market Institutions," pp. 160–62.

33. Juliet B. Schor makes a related argument in *The Overspent American* (New York: Basic Books, 1998).

34. Ethan Bronner, "College Freshmen Aiming for High Marks in Income," *New York Times,* January 12, 1998, p. A11.

35. A more benign, and to some extent surely valid, explanation is that rising enrollment rates mean that today's freshmen include more young people from families who have never experienced financial comfort, and who consequently weight it higher.

36. A freshman charting his course in 1968, with as much rationality as an eighteen-year-old can muster, might notice that joining the richest 5 percent of families, the likely prize for unrelenting practicality, meant average annual income of about $30,000 (or around $128,000 in 1996 dollars). If he was slightly less focused in his course of studies, or slightly less earnings-conscious in his choice of a mate, or slightly less lucky, and only made it into the top one-fifth instead of the top twentieth, he might expect family income of just under $20,000 ($82,000 in 1996 dollars), or about one-third less. And if he was so preoccupied with "developing a meaningful philosophy of life" that despite his initial advantages he ended up with only average family income, that average would be about $8,600 (worth $36,000 in 1996). Consider his counterpart in 1996. The same operative definition of "being very well off financially"—membership in the top 5 percent of families—now meant an average annual income of a little over $217,000. The difference between this top prize and the consolation prize of top-fifth family income (averaging $125,000) was a good deal greater than it had been in 1968. But the real difference for the 1997 freshman concerned the consequences of ending up in the middle of the income distribution (not to mention below the middle) if she worried too little about her financial future. The average income for middle-fifth families, nearly $42,500, was more, by a bit, than her father could have anticipated in parallel circumstances, but dramatically less than the top prize. And if every risk turned sour and she ended up in the bottom fifth of families, her income would be only one-twentieth that of her more prudent classmates who ended up in the top 5 percent—double the worst-case penalty her 1968 counterpart confronted. (Family income data are from *Historical Data from the Current Population Survey,* Table F–3.)

37. Quotation from Peter Gay, *Pleasure Wars: The Bourgeois Experience,* vol. 5 (New York: W.W. Norton, 1998), review by Roger Shattuck in *New York Times Book Review*, February 1, 1998, p. 11.

38. Many people at lower levels of the income spectrum, of course, would prefer to have higher incomes, likely even if that meant less income for those at the top. Some might wish that top incomes declined even if their own stayed the same, so that they are no longer priced out of the market for scarce commodities like housing in desirable cities, admission to top schools, or even political influence. Some might even accept lower income themselves as part of a package including narrower disparities, to ease a sense of relative deprivation or to mend a culture tilted too far toward materialism. Not all of the less favored would prefer such changes, to be sure. Some lower-income people like the idea of high earnings at the top because they fully expect to make it to the top by and by; some cherish the dream of riches even if they find its fulfillment remote; and some simply feel that other people's income is none of their business.

3

1. U.S. Treasury Department, Office of State and Local Finance, *Federal-State-Local Fiscal Relations: Report to the President and the Congress*, Washington, D.C., September 1985, p. vii.

2. R. Kent Newmyer, "John Marshall, Political Parties, and the Origins of Modern Federalism," in Harry N. Scheiber, ed., *Federalism: Studies in History, Law, and Public Policy* (Berkeley, Calif.: Institute of Inter-governmental Studies, 1988), p. 19.

3. *McCulloch v. Maryland*, 17 U.S. 316 (1816) granted Congress an expansive definition of the "necessary and proper" clause in Article I. *Gibbons v. Ogden*, 22 U.S. 1 (1824) launched the use of the commerce clause as the predicate for federal activism.

4. Garry Wills claims to have pinpointed the precise time and manner of its occurrence—November 19, 1863, in the passionate evocation of national identity and purpose compressed into Abraham Lincoln's Gettysburg Address. See Garry Wills "The Words That Remade America: Lincoln at Gettysburg," *Atlantic Monthly*, June 1992. Whether or not Lincoln's words exercised such *specific* leverage over history, the accumulation of federal power in the post-Civil War era cannot be denied.

5. Harold Laski, in a famous 1938 article, amplified themes struck earlier by Herbert Croly when he argued that the imperative of a centralized governmental response to a centralized modern capitalism meant that "the epoch of federalism is over." "The Obsolescence of Federalism," *New Republic*, May 3, 1938, p. 367.

6. See Thomas R. Swartz and John E. Peck, "The Changing Face of Fiscal Federalism," *Challenge* 33, no. 6 (November–December 1990): 42–43.

7. U.S. Department of Commerce, *Statistical Abstract of the United States 1992* (Washington, D.C.: U.S. Government Printing Office, 1993), Table 470, p. 282.

8. There are different ways of counting the number of block grants and consolidated programs. This tally is from the General Accounting Office, in Block Grants: Lessons Learned (Testimony, February 9, 1995, GAO/T-HEHS-95-80).

9. Robert Pear, "Source of State Power Is Pulled from Ashes," *New York Times*, April 19, 1995.

10. The Clinton quote is from remarks delivered to the Democratic Governors' Association in Washington, D.C., and distributed by the White House Office of the Press Secretary, February 5, 1996.

11. From the on–line version of the Democratic platform posted on the Democratic National Committee website August 19, 1996 (www.dncc96.org/ platform).

12. The Gallup and Roper polls from the 1930s are summarized in Robert J. Blendon et al., "Changing Attitudes in America," September 1996 photocopy (provided to author by Robert Blendon), Table 6.

13. The Gallup Poll, *Public Opinion 1995* (Princeton, N.J.: The Gallup Organization, 1996), pp. 143–49, 213.

14. Hart and Teeter Poll, conducted March 1995 for the Council for Excellence in Government, on the council website (www.excelgov.org/htpoll). A 1997 poll by Hart and Teeter, also for the council, affirmed the continuing edge of state and local government in citizens' esteem. The 1997 poll is at www.excelgov.org/hart.

15. November–December 1995 survey, Princeton Survey Research Associates for Washington Post, Kaiser Family Foundation, and Harvard University, as summarized by Blendon et al., "Changing Attitudes in America." The gap reflects more a loss of confidence in the federal government than any great enthusiasm for the states; while 75 percent trust the federal government to "do the right thing" only some of the time or never, 64 percent are similarly skeptical of their state governments. A mid-1998 poll conducted for the Pew Charitable Trusts produced a similar pattern of greater trust in state than in federal government.

16. P.L. 104-4 is discussed in "Unfunded Mandate Bill Highlights," *Congressional Quarterly Almanac 1995* (Washington, D.C.: Congressional Quarterly, 1995), pp. 3–17.

17. Robert Pear, "White House Plans Medicaid Coverage of Viagra by States," *New York Times*, May 28, 1998, p. 1

18. These figures are from the FY 1999 federal budget proposal compiled in U.S. Office of Management and Budget, *Budget of the United States Government, Fiscal Year 1999* (Washington, D.C.: U.S. Government Printing Office, 1997), Historical Table 15.5 (www.acc-ess.gpo/ su_docs/budget99/ hist15.5_wk1).

19. These OMB data commingle state and local spending and hence can't confirm, on their own, the states' ascendancy. But a different data series collected by the Census Bureau tracks state and local finances separately. Over 1960–64, state spending averaged only a little over one-third of the state and local total. Over 1990–93, it exceeded one-half. It is chiefly the states, and not the cities, that are waxing as Washington wanes. Nor do the OMB data disaggregate nonfederal spending to isolate the growing role of transfer payments. Figure 3.1 thus overstates somewhat the relative importance of state and local *operations*, since transfers are not netted out as they are for the federal figures. The National Income and Product Accounts data *do* track transfers separately. They show that AFDC, Medicaid, and other transfer programs have risen steadily as a share of state spending, from under 20 percent in the early 1960s to around 30 percent in the early 1990s. Yet the NIPA data underscore the prominence of lower-level governments in running things, as distinct from writing checks. In 1995, transfers claimed less than half as large a share of state and local budgets as they did of federal budgets.

4

1. "Devolution," strictly speaking, refers to the formal transfer of responsibilities to lower levels of government. This is only part, and not the largest part, of the shift toward the states at issue here.

2. These state figures were calculated from data graciously supplied by Jon Haveman of Purdue University and the Council of Economic Advisors. The relatively small size of a single state sample makes the estimates somewhat shaky, and not too much should be made of the precise value for any particular state. But the general picture of widely varying inequality from one state to another is certainly accurate. A separate compilation of state-by-state income inequality by researchers at the Center for Budget and Policy Priorities uses a slightly different time period and restricts itself to families with children. By their methodology, the list of least-equal states started with New York, Louisiana, New Mexico, Arizona, and Connecticut, slightly different from Haveman's top five of Louisiana, California, New York, Mississippi, and New Mexico. The four most-equal states are the same by both methods (Utah, North Dakota, Vermont, and Wisconsin); Haveman ranks Montana next, the center researchers rank Iowa next. For the most part, the two methods generate similar rankings. Kathryn Larin and Elizabeth McNichol, *Pulling Apart: A State-by-State Analysis of Income Trends*, Center on Budget and Policy Priorities, December 1997, http://www.cbpp.org/pa-1.htm.

3. One dimension of difference, not taken up here, concerns the advantages of simplicity and homogeneity when decisions are made "close to the people," balanced against the risks of factional dominance that worried James Madison. Related issues are discussed in John D. Donahue, *Disunited States* (New York: Basic Books, 1997), especially Chapter 3.

5

1. Revenue share figures are calculated from U.S. Office of Management and Budget, *Budget of the United States Government Fiscal Year 1999* (Washington, D.C.: U.S. Government Printing Office, 1997), Historical Table 15.1 (www.access.gov/su_docs/budget99/hist15.1_wk1).

2. Income tax data are from Therese Cruciano, "Individual Income Tax Rates and Tax Shares 1994," Internal Revenue Service, *Statistics of Income Bulletin* (Spring 1997), Figure B, p. 9.

3. Advisory Commission on Intergovernmental Relations, *Significant Features of Fiscal Federalism 1995* (Washington, D.C.: Advisory Commission on Intergovernmental Relations, September 1995).

4. Averaging over the 1988–94 period, Americans age twenty-five and over with family income between $25,000 and $50,000 had about a 2.4 percent probability of moving interstate in a given year, while those with incomes over $50,000 had about a 3.0 percent probability. Calculated from U.S. Department of Commerce, Bureau of the Census, *Current Population Reports* (Washington D.C.: U.S. Government Printing Office, various years), P-20 series. While mobility rates vary from year to year, at no time over the period were higher-income people less likely to move interstate than middle-income people.

5. Calculated from Kristen A. Hansen, "Geographical Mobility: March 1993 to March 1994," *Current Population Reports* (Washington, D.C.: U.S. Department of Commerce, August 1995), Table 1.

6. George F. Break, *Intergovernmental Fiscal Relations in the United States* (Washington, D.C.: Brookings Institution Press, 1967), pp. 23–24. A more recent literature review also finds a "tendency for interjurisdictional competition to reduce reliance on ability-to-pay taxes." Advisory Commission on Intergovernmental Relations, *Interjurisdictional Tax and Policy Competition: Good or Bad for the Federal System?* (Washington, D.C.: Advisory Commission on Intergovernmental Relations, April 1991), p. 63.

7. One analyst found that by most measures, all state tax codes are regressive, and only Delaware is progressive by any measure. Donald W. Keifer, "A Comparative Analysis of Tax Progressivity in the United States: A Reexamination," *Public Finance Quarterly* 19, no. 1 (January 1991).

8. Some of the evidence and arguments concerning the effects of taxation and other state policies on business location are summarized in the appendix of John D. Donahue, *Disunited States* (New York: Basic Books, 1997), pp. 171–82.

9. Corina Eckl and Arturo Perez, *State Budget Actions 1997* (Denver and Washington, D.C.: National Council of State Legislatures, December 1997), pp. 4–5, incl. Figure 1.

10. "Average Sales Tax Rates Reach Record High," Vertex Inc. press release, Vertex, Berwyn, Pa., January 1997

11. Early 1990s baseline calculated from data in U.S. Department of Commerce, Bureau of the Census, Governments Division, on-line compilation, "Quarterly State and Local Tax Data," Table 2, "National Totals of State Tax Revenue, by Type of Tax" (www.census.gov/govs/qtax/qtx981); the 1995–97 tax-cut aggregates are calculated (using the NCSL's "taxpayer liability" method) from *State Tax Actions* (Louisville, Ky.: National Council of State Legislatures, 1995, 1996, and 1997 issues). The sales tax category combines general sales taxes (which were reduced, on balance, over the period) with special sales taxes, which were increased.

12. *State Tax Actions 1997*, Appendix H, pp. 35–37.

6

1. For some early commentary on welfare reform, see Robyn Meredith, "Michigan Welfare Plan Draws Unlikely Support," *New York Times*, January 22, 1996; Jason Deparle, "Aid from an Enemy of the Welfare State," *New York Times,* January 28, 1996; Jennifer Preston, "Whitman Proposes Welfare Plan Intended to Ease a Shift to Work," *New York Times*, January 30, 1996; Gordon Mermin and C. Eugene Steuerle, "The Impact of TANF on State Budgets," Washington, D.C., Urban Institute, November 1997; L. Jerome Gallagher et al., "One Year after Federal Welfare Reform: A Description of State Temporary Assistance for Needy Families Decisions as of October 1997," Washington, D.C., Urban Institute, June 1998; and the compendium of press reports on state responses to welfare reform collected in "Reporting from the Trenches," *Washington Monthly*, January–February 1998, pp. 35–39. The Urban Institute, among other major organizations, has mounted a vast empirical effort to inform eventual evaluation of welfare devolution.

2. Paul E. Peterson and Mark Rom, "American Federalism, Welfare Policy, and Residential Choices," *American Political Science Review* 83, no. 3 (September 1989): 724.

3. The 1940–85 reference is from ibid., p. 715; the Clinton quote is from "Clinton Okays Changes to Welfare," Reuters on-line wire, July 16, 1996.

4. Phillip B. Levine and David Zimmerman use longitudinal data to test whether welfare-eligible families are more likely than others to move to high-benefit states, and conclude that welfare is a minor factor in migration patterns. "An Empirical Analysis of the Welfare Magnet Debate Using the NLSY," NBER Working Paper No. 5264, Cambridge, Mass., September 1995. Edward M. Gramlich and Deborah S. Laren, using somewhat different methods and data series, find a small but measurable "welfare magnet" effect. While the poor (like most people) move out of state only rarely, when they *do* move it is more likely to a high-benefits state. From the 1960s through the mid-1980s Gramlich and Laren see a "very sluggish migration process toward high-benefit states, which is gradually reducing the real level of AFDC benefits as it becomes perceived." "Migration and Income Redistribution Responsibilities," *Journal of Human Resources* 19, no. 4 (1984): 509. For the entire 1900–87 period, two scholars find "strong statistical evidence that, all else being equal, higher per-capita income leads to a greater rate of net in-migration" for population overall. Robert J. Barro and Xavier Sala-I-Martin, "Convergence across States and Regions," *Brookings Papers on Economic Activity,* no. 1 (1991): 132.

5. For references to California and Wisconsin, see Sam Howe Verhovek, "States Are Already Providing Glimpse at Welfare's Future," *New York*

Times, September 21, 1995; for references to New York, see Kenneth B. Noble, "Welfare Revamp, Halted in Capital, Proceeds Anyway," *New York Times,* March 10, 1996, and Raymond Hernandez, "Pataki's Plans for Welfare: Strict Rules and Job Incentives," *New York Times,* February 6, 1996. Shortly before the welfare reform bill became effective a New York state senator sought to assemble a coalition for reforming the state's constitution to limit antipoverty efforts, warning that "delay may well be cataclysmic. Thousands of poor Americans from other states could trek to New York. . . ." John J. Marchi, "New York's Welfare Meltdown," *New York Times,* August 12, 1996, op-ed. According to Paul Peterson, "Massachusetts has reported that welfare recipients are already leaving the state in response to cuts enacted in the spring of 1995." *The Price of Federalism* (Washington, D.C.: Brookings Institution, 1995), p. 187.

6. The federal entitlement ended as of October 1, 1996 (though states had nine months to submit their plans for meeting the terms of the legislation and collecting their block grants). But Wisconsin, Michigan, Ohio, Florida, Vermont, Massachusetts, Maryland, Oregon, Oklahoma, Tennessee, and Maine submitted their plans earlier, and Wisconsin and Michigan had been approved—that is, certified as consistent with the reform legislation, the only criterion for approval—the evening before the law became effective. Robert Pear, "Actions by States Hold Keys to Welfare Law's Future," *New York Times,* October 1, 1996.

7. Kevin Sack, "In Mississippi, Will Poor Grow Poorer with State Welfare Plans?" *New York Times,* October 23, 1995.

8. Mickey Kaus, "The Revival of Liberalism," *New York Times,* August 9, 1996.

9. The late Stephen Gold, then director for the Center for the Study of the States and later director of a major research effort on the impact of devolution, assessed Michigan's plan bluntly in 1995. "You can see they're not going to have enough money. They will say, 'Well, we can't raise taxes, so we will have to cut spending more.' They are sowing the seeds of further cuts in social spending." Peter Kilborne, "Michigan's Welfare System: Praise Amid Warning Signs," *New York Times,* October 24, 1995. Robert Reischauer, former director of the Congressional Budget Office and later a Brookings Institution researcher, predicts that the shift to block grants will cause state spending on vulnerable populations to "drop like a rock." "The Blockbuster Inside the Republicans' Budget: In the Rush to Fiscal Devolution, Has Anyone Figured Out How to Divvy Up the Cash?" In *Dollars and Sense: Diverse Perspectives on Block Grants and the Fiscal Responsibility Act* (Washington, D.C.: Institute for Educational Leadership, September 1995), p. 60.

10. The nineteenth-century English poor laws restricted paupers' mobility to make decentralized poor relief sustainable, which is not an option for

modern America. The 1996 reform legislation gave states some tools for restricting the immigration of potential aid recipients, but early court tests cast doubt on their workability. *(Shortly before this essay went to press the Supreme Court definitely blocked such tactics.)* On the poor laws see Karl Polanyi, *The Great Transformation* (Boston: Beacon Press, 1944). Relevant U.S. court cases include *Shapiro v. Thompson,* 394 U.S. 618 (1969) and *Memorial Hospital v. Maricopa County,* 415 U.S. 250 (1974). It is interesting to note, in this regard, that the Articles of Confederation specifically exclude "paupers" from the provision that "the people of each state shall have free ingress and regress to and from any other state." Article IV, *Articles of Confederation,* from Samuel Eliot Morison, ed., *Sources and Documents Illustrating the American Revolution* (London: Oxford University Press, 1923), p. 178.

7

1. Senator Kassebaum's comments are from the *Daily Labor Report,* December 18, 1995.

2. States with minimum wages exceeding the federal minimum are from Richard R. Nelson, "State Labor Legislation Enacted in 1996," *Monthly Labor Review,* January 1997, p. 29; the District of Columbia is excluded. State rankings by annual average pay are from Bureau of Labor Statistics data assembled in *Statistical Abstract of the United States, 1997,* Table 669. Both because the reference is to annual, rather than hourly, pay, and because the analysis here is decidedly informal, I term the proposition that states can maintain binding minimum wages "debatable" rather than flatly wrong, and more careful research would be required to settle the point.

3. Technically, the legislation mandates a comprehensive and expensive *national* system of unemployment insurance, but allows states enacting their own systems to opt out of the national arrangements—which all states have done.

4. It is debatable whether the premiums are actually paid by corporate shareholders—the apparent bearers of the burden—or by workers, in the form of lower wages. A strong conceptual case can be made that workers will ultimately foot the bill, but in principle firms tend to call for leaner UI systems and workers for richer ones, suggesting either that managers and workers don't know what's good for them or that there are flaws in the theoretical story.

5. Lauri J. Bassi et al., "The Evolution of Unemployment Insurance," Advisory Council on Unemployment Compensation staff paper, August 1995, Table 1, p. 3.

6. Ibid., p. 28.

7. Ibid., p. 11.

8. A comparable syndrome of competitive austerity has been under way with workers' compensation, where states have been increasing the scrutiny injury claims receive and limiting the benefits to which workers hurt on the job are entitled. But this trend has been driven in part by honest concerns about fraud, as well as by states' anxieties to accommodate mobile capital.

9. See *The New Democrat*'s special issue on "Why America Needs a New Labor," *The New Democrat* 10, no. 2 (March/April 1998).

10. This list draws on David T. Elwood and Glenn Fine, "The Impact of Right-to-Work Laws on Union Organizing," *Journal of Political Economy* 95, no. 2 (1987), especially Table 1, p. 251.

11. This literature is summarized in William J. Moore and Robert J. Newman, "The Effects of Right-to-Work Laws: A Review of the Literature," *Industrial and Labor Relations Review*, July 1985.

12. Richard Ruback and Martin Zimmerman, "Unionization and Profitability: Evidence from the Capital Market," *Journal of Political Economy* (December 1984), cited in Steven E. Abraham and Paula B. Voos, "Right to Work Laws: New Evidence from the Stock Market" (photocopy supplied to author July 1997), p. 16.

13. Abraham and Voos, "Right to Work Laws."

14. Ellwood and Fine, "Impact of Right-to-Work Laws," esp. pp. 270–71.

15. The membership rate is for wage and salary workers; the 1983 figure is from the *Statistical Abstract of the United States,* and the 1997 figure is from a Bureau of Labor Statistics press release, January 30, 1998, at http://stats.bls.gov/newsrels.htm.

8

1. Lynn A. Karoly, "Anatomy of the U.S. Income Distribution: Two Decades of Change," *Oxford Review of Economic Policy* 12, no. 1 (1996): 84, Table 2. Shifts in family structure—such as the tendency of single parents to be less educated, or of college-educated men to marry college-educated working women, intensify the trend, but rising returns to education are a major part of the story.

2. For a sample of this debate, see Eric A. Hanushek, "The Economics of Schooling: Production and Efficiency in Public Schools," *Journal of Economic Literature* 24 (September 1986); David Card and Alan B. Krueger, "School Resources and Student Outcomes: An Overview of the Literature and New Evidence from North and South Carolina," *Journal of Economic*

Perspectives 10, no. 4 (Fall 1996); and Gary Burtless, ed., *Does Money Matter? The Effect of School Resources on Student Achievement and Adult Success* (Washington, D.C.: Brookings Institution Press, 1996).

3. Corina Eckl, "Let the Good Times Roll!" *State Legislatures* (October/November 1997): 25–26.

4. Tamar Lewin, "States Appear Ready to Raise Their Spending on Education," *New York Times,* March 16, 1998.

5. Tamar Lewin, "Patchwork of School Financing Schemes Offers Few Answers and Much Conflict," *New York Times,* April 8, 1998.

6. Richard Perez-Pena, "Spending, Not Tax-Cutting, Draws Focus of 3 Governors," *New York Times,* February 20, 1998.

7. These enrollment figures and projections are from the National Center for Education Statistics, *Digest of Education Statistics 1996,* Table 3, "Enrollment in Educational Institutions, by Level and by Control of Institution: 1869–70 to Fall 2006" (nces.ed.gov/ pubs/d96/D96T003).

8. Thomas J. Kane is a leading researcher on the link between cost and college access for less affluent youth. His paper, "Rising Public College Tuition and College Entry: How Well Do Public Subsidies Promote Access to College?" (National Bureau of Economic Research Working Paper No. 5164, July 1995), is a particularly good source. College enrollment rates for eighteen- and nineteen-year-olds vary dramatically by family income. Over the 1977–93 period around 70 percent of eighteen- and nineteen-year-olds from top-quartile families have attended postsecondary institutions, with the rate rising more recently. The second-highest and second-lowest quartiles generally display enrollment rates a little above and a little below 50 percent, respectively. And enrollment rates for youth from the bottom quartile start below 30 percent and actually drift downward as college attendance for more affluent youth is rising, especially in the early 1990s. (Figure 2, appendix.) Kane makes use of the fact that tuition ranges widely among states, and that some states (such as Massachusetts) have sharply increased tuition, to see whether tuition increases and aid reductions are pricing some young people out of the market. He suggests that about one-fifth of the growing discrepancies in enrollment rates is due to tuition increases at state two-year colleges (p. 3).

9. Figures from Steven D. Gold, "Issues Raised by the New Federalism," *National Tax Journal* 49, no. 2 (June 1996) 283.

10. Aside from tax-limit statutes and growing skepticism about the efficiency of public education, we can expect demographic trends to put growing downward pressure on local revenues for the schools as the older baby boomers move out of their child-rearing years and the elderly population grows. For thoughtful research on this last factor see James M. Poterba, "Demographic Structure and the Political Economy of Public Education," *Policy Analysis and Management* 16, no. 1 (Winter 1997).

11. Office of Management and Budget, *Budget of the United States, Fiscal Year 1998* (Washington, D.C.: Government Printing Office, 1998), Table 8.8. Real education spending is anticipated to decline slightly after a peak in FY 1999.

12. This calculation is based on figures from U.S. Department of Education, National Center for Education Statistics, *Digest of Education Statistics 1997* (Washington, D.C.: Government Printing Office, 1997), Table 2.

13. As recently as 1995, categorical grants accounted for 90 percent of federal transfers to states and localities. R. Kent Weaver, "Deficits and Devolution in the 104th Congress," *Publius* (Summer 1996) 47.

14. These figures are from the Census Bureau's Governments Division on-line data compilation for 1996 (http://www. census.gov/ govs/state/96stus.txt), accessed in May 1998.

15. See the references above to Thomas Kane's work on tuition increases and discrepant postsecondary enrollment rates. Figure 8.7 is not directly comparable to Figure 8.6, because it presents spending in nominal rather than inflation-adjusted terms.

16. Jay Mathews, "Corporations Vow to Favor States That Boost Academic Standards," *Washington Post,* March 28, 1996.

17. Antonio Ciccone and Robert E. Hall, "Productivity and the Density of Economic Activity," *American Economic Review* 86, no. 1 (March 1996), esp. p. 54 and Figure 2, p. 64. This is the most recent and prestigious study of the issue. Most, but not all, empiricists agree on the importance of education for productivity. One provocative but ultimately not very plausible regression study found that a state's level of education spending was inversely related to short-term economic growth rates in the mid-1970s. Thomas R. Dye, "Taxing, Spending and Economic Growth in American States," *Journal of Politics* 42 (1980): 1100, Table.

18. See Gold, "Issues Raised by the New Federalism," on this point.

19. These averages are based on data from U.S. Department of Commerce, *Current Population Reports,* P-20 Series (Washington, D.C: U.S. Government Printing Office, various annual issues).

20. Data for 1995 to 1996 show 1.5 percent of adult high-school dropouts and 3.1 percent of college graduates moving out of state. Calculated from Table 5, Kristen A. Hansen, "Geographical Mobility March 1995 to March 1996," *Current Population Reports,* November 1997.

21. Robert Tomsho, "Rio Rancho Wooed Industry and Got It, Plus Financial Woes," *Wall Street Journal,* April 11, 1995.

22. Claudia Goldin and Lawrence F. Katz, "The Decline of Non-Competing Groups: Changes in the Premium to Education, 1880 to 1940,"

NBER Working Paper No. 5202 (Washington, D.C.: National Bureau of Economic Research, August 1995), p. 30.

23. Stanley Elkins and Erik McKitrick, *The Age of Federalism* (New York and Oxford: Oxford University Press, 1993), p. 198.

9

1. In 1994–95, total government spending on all levels of education was about $350 billion, of which federal spending accounted for $44 billion, or about 12.5 percent. The federal share of government financing is lowest (about 7.5 percent) for public primary and secondary schools and highest (about 84 percent) for private postsecondary institutions. These figures exclude federal tax expenditures and tuition assistance. See *Digest of Education Statistics 1997,* Table 33, "Estimated Total Expenditures of Educational Institutions, by Level, Control of Institution, and Source of Funds: 1979–80 to 1994–95" (nces.ed.gov/pubs/digest97/d97t033).

2. Reserve Board Flow of Funds, Table B.100, "Balance Sheet of Household and Nonprofit Sector, March 1998," on-line data from http://stat-usa.gov/BEN/ebb1/frb/z1. These figures include real and financial holdings of nonprofit organizations, but household assets dominate the totals.

3. For wealth distribution data from the Panel Study of Income Dynamics, see Erik Hurst, Ming Ching Luoh, and Frank P. Stafford, "Wealth Dynamics of American Families, 1984–1994," Department of Economics and Institute for Social Research, University of Michigan, Ann Arbor, August 1996, esp. Table 2. Even by this PSID measure, which is more likely to miss the wealthiest families than other tabulations of wealth, the top 10 percent held about 69 percent of property other than main residences, but only 59 percent when homes are included.

4. The *use* of owner-occupied real estate—an analogue of the return on financial investment—is also generally untaxed.

5. A tally of 1995 property tax rates in fifty-one cities, adjusted for peculiarities of valuation that can make nominal rates misleadingly high, ranges from 0.33 percent to 4.75 percent, with an average of 1.78 percent and most cities in the 1.0 to 2.0 percent range; U.S. Department of Commerce, Bureau of the Census, *Statistical Abstract of the United States 1997* (Washington, D.C.: U.S. Government Printing Office, 1998), Table 497.

6. Edward N. Wolff, "How the Pie Is Sliced," *American Prospect* 22 (Summer 1995): 58–64 (http://epn.org/prospect/22/22wolf.html).

7. The 1964–95 lottery figure, $52 billion earmarked for education for all states together, is from U.S. Department of Commerce, Bureau of the Census, *Statistical Abstract of the United States 1997* (Washington, D.C.: U.S. Government Printing Office, 1998), Table 499.

INDEX

ABOUT THE AUTHOR

John D. Donahue is an associate professor at Harvard's John F. Kennedy School of Government. Most of his teaching, writing, and research deals with the allocation of responsibilities across levels of government and between the public and private sectors. His book, *Disunited States* (Basic Books, 1997), explores the shift toward the separate states in American government's center of gravity. He is also the author of *The Privatization Decision: Public Ends, Private Means* (Basic Books, 1991), which has been published in five languages, and the coauthor (with Robert B. Reich) of *New Deals: The Chrysler Revival and the American System* (Times Books, 1986). His shorter writings have appeared in the *Atlantic Monthly,* the *Journal of Economic Perspectives,* the *American Prospect,* and other publications. He held senior policy posts at the U.S. Department of Labor during the first Clinton administration and helped to frame initiatives on job training reform and education tax incentives. He lives in Lexington, Massachusetts, with his wife, Maggie Pax, and their young children, Kate and Ben.